COOKING
LIKE A

GODDESS

Me at fourteen, absently stirring something on the stove with my nose buried in a book (my usual cooking stance). That's my mother the Kitchen Goddess on the right.

COOKING
LIKE A
GODDESS

Bringing Seasonal Magic into the Kitchen

CAIT JOHNSON

MONOPRINT COLLAGES BY JOHANNE RENBECK

Healing Arts Press
Rochester, Vermont

Healing Arts Press
One Park Street
Rochester, Vermont 05767
www.gotoit.com

*Note to the reader: This book is intended as an informational guide. The remedies, approaches,
and techniques described herein are meant to supplement, and not to be a substitute for, professional medical care or treatment.
They should not be used to treat a serious ailment without prior consultation with a qualified health-care professional.*

"How to Stuff a Pepper" from *Carpenter of the Sun* by Nancy Willard. Copyright © 1974 by Nancy Willard.
Reprinted by permission of Liveright Publishing Corporation.

Excerpt from *Carmina Gadelica* by Alexander Carmichael used by permission of Lindisfarne Books, Hudson, NY 12534.

Illustrations on pages 38, 57, 80, 101, 126, 133, 166, and 180 copyright © 1997 by Johanne Renbeck.

Library of Congress Cataloging-in-Publication Data
Johnson, Cait.
Cooking like a goddess : bringing seasonal magic
into the kitchen / Cait Johnson ; illustrations by Johanne Renbeck.
p.   cm.
Includes bibliographical references (p.   ) and index.
ISBN 0-89281-739-9 (alk. paper)
1. Cookery. 2. Cookery—Religious aspects. I. Title.
TX714.J598 1997   97-24158
641.5—dc21   CIP

Printed and bound in the United States

10   9   8   7   6   5   4   3   2   1

Text design and layout by Virginia L. Scott

This book was typeset in Weiss and Frutiger with Schneidler Initials, Garamond Expert,
and Bauer Text Initials as the display typefaces

Healing Arts Press is a division of Inner Traditions International

Distributed to the book trade in Canada by Publishers Group West (PGW), Toronto, Ontario
Distributed to the health food trade in Canada by Alive Books, Toronto and Vancouver
Distributed to the book trade in the United Kingdom by Deep Books, London
Distributed to the book trade in Australia by Millennium Books, Newtown, N.S.W.
Distributed to the book trade in New Zealand by Tandem Press, Auckland
Distributed to the book trade in South Africa by Alternative Books, Ferndale

Dedicated to the nourishing Goddess:
may her rising heal and feed us all.

For my mother, Patricia Johnson,
who has always been a goddess in the kitchen,
and for Maura D. Shaw,
great nurturer, mentor, and friend.

For thousands of years, the feminine in the form of a hearth or fire goddess was central to many cultures. Known by many names, her energy was remarkably consistent around the world. She was the keeper of the hearth and the knower of the spiritual nature of human beings. She was a doorway into the inner world of the soul.

Anne Scott,
Serving Fire

My connection to the natural world is my connection to self—erotic, mysterious, and whole.

Terry Tempest Williams,
An Unspoken Hunger

I give myself over to this gift.
I adorn this table with food.
I invite lovers and friends to come share.
I thank you for this gift.
All that I have comes from my Mother!

Luisa Teish,
Jambalaya

CONTENTS

Acknowledgments   xiii
Introduction   1

ONE
KITCHEN MAGIC

Making Your Kitchen a Sacred Space   6
Putting Down Roots   9
  Cleaning   10
  The Power Place   15
  Convenience   17
  Allies in the Kitchen   17
  Creativity   20
  Community   20
The Kitchen Altar   21
  Kitchen Goddesses   22
  Placement   23
  Honoring Who You Are   24
  Ancestor Feasts   25
  Decoration   25
  Consecration   27
  The Kitchen Goddess Feast   27
Making a Kitchen Goddess Apron   28
  Apron Decoration   29

For the Very Bold   32

Kitchen Rituals   33

    Kitchen of the Goddess   35

TWO

THE EARTH MOTHER'S SEASONS

AUTUMN   39

    Setting the Stage for Autumn   40

    The Autumn Kitchen   41

    Song of the Early Autumn Goddess   44

Early Autumn Recipes   46

    Apple-Squash Soup   46

    Nutty Autumn Salads   47

    Crisp Corn Tarts with Autumn
      Greens and Hazelnuts   48

    Three Sisters Harvest Stew   50

    Simple Baked Pears   52

    Song of the Midautumn Goddess   53

    Kitchen Rituals for the Autumn Equinox   54

    Pomegranate Meditation   56

Midautumn Recipes   59

    Demeter's Soothing Oat-Bread Soup   59

    Persephone Salad   61

    Persephone's Autumn Dressing   62

    Autumn Chard   62

    Creamy Cashew Sauce   63

    Stuffed Acorn Squash   64

    Fig-Apple Crumble   66

    Song of the Late Autumn Goddess   67

    Kitchen Rituals for Samhain   68

      Scrying Brew   69

Late Autumn Recipes 72

   Cailleach (Kale-Leek) Soup 72

   Apple Salad 73

   Autumn Cider Dressing 74

   Sweet Potato–Apple Bake 75

   Lovable Lentils in Pumpkin Bowls 76

   Moony Apple Pie 77

   Classic No-Dairy Crust 78

   Last Word of the Autumn Goddess 79

WINTER 81

   Setting the Stage for Winter 82

   The Winter Kitchen 83

   Story of the Early Winter Goddess 87

Early Winter Recipes 89

   How to Cook a Pumpkin 89

   Things to Do with Cooked Pumpkin 91

   Smoky Pumpkin Soup 92

   Winter Greens and Walnuts Salad 93

   Heartha's Roasted Winter Vegetables 94

   Kale, Corn, and Onion Skillet Cakes 96

   Pumpkin Pudding (or Pie) 97

   Story of the Midwinter Goddess 98

   Midwinter Meditation: Eating the Earth 100

   Kitchen Rituals for Winter Solstice 103

     White Pine Tea 105

     Wassail 106

Midwinter Recipes 108

   Root Soup 108

   Pomander Salad 109

   Pomander Dressing 110

   Festive Green Beans with Cranberries 110

   Savory Yuletide Pie 111

Plum Pudding   114
Story of the Late Winter Goddess   116
Late Winter Recipes   118
Thousand-Names Bean Soup   118
Rooted Winter Salads   120
Winter Sunset Carrots   122
Leek and Potato Gratin   122
Winter Fruit Pies   124
Last Word of the Winter Goddess   125

SPRING   127
Setting the Stage for Spring   128
The Spring Kitchen   129
Film of the Early Spring Goddess   131
Sprouting Meditation   132
The Sprouting Experience   134
Embodying the Spring   135
Kitchen Rituals for Imbolc   136
Maura's Irish Soda Bread   138
Early Spring Recipes   139
Brigid's Broth of Inspiration   139
Sprouted Spring Salads   141
Spring Greens   142
Magic Isle Pasties   142
Waking Earth Cake   144
Film of the Midspring Goddess   146
Kitchen Rituals for Spring Equinox   146
Midspring Recipes   149
Ukemochi Miso Soup   149
Salad Nests   150
Ume Plum Dressing   151

New Potatoes with Dill 151

Spring Supper Omelet with Mushrooms 152

Maple Candy 153

Film of the Late Spring Goddess 155

Kitchen Rituals for Beltane 156

Late Spring Recipes 157

Sensuous Spinach Soup 157

Wild Salad 158

Beltane Asparagus 160

Toasted Tamari Almonds 161

Risotto Primavera 161

Aphrodite's Love Cakes 163

Last Word of the Spring Goddess 165

SUMMER 167

Setting the Stage for Summer 168

The Summer Kitchen 169

Dance of the Early Summer Goddess 170

Early Summer Recipes 171

Goddess's Green Pea Soup 171

Flowering Salad 172

Simple Summer Dressing 173

Daylily-Bud Sauté 174

Juno's Summer Quiche 175

Wholemeal Crust 176

Simple Strawberry Shortcake 177

Whole Wheat Shortcake Squares 178

Dance of the Midsummer Goddess 179

Tasty Midsummer Recipe-Meditation 179

Hot Summer Peach-Play for Lovers 181

Kitchen Rituals for Summer Solstice 182

Midsummer Recipes   184
   Titania's Cherry Soup   184
   Midsummer Salad   185
   Smoky Summer Vegetables on the Grill   186
   Midsummer Marinades   187
     Hot Mama Marinade   187
     Sweet and Tangy Marinade   187
     Herbed Red Wine Marinade   188
   Things to Do with Grilled Vegetables   188
   Fiery Red Beans and Rice   189
   Enchanted Berries   191
   Dance of the Late Summer Goddess   192
   Kitchen Rituals for First Harvest   193
   Real Earth-Mother Whole Grain Bread   194
   Shuck Bread   196
Late Summer Recipes   198
   Tomato Venus Soup   198
   Crunchy Summer Salads   199
   Simple-Gifts Millet   200
   Mama Zabetta's Spicy Stir-Fried Greens   201
   Sunny Peach Pie   203
   Graham Cracker Crust   204
   Last Word of the Summer Goddess   204

Wild Woman Tips for Acting Out in
  the Kitchen   205
Suggested Reading   208
Supplies   216
Index   219

ACKNOWLEDGMENTS

To the pantheon of Great Ones who were especially involved in this project, my devoted thanks: Artemis of Ephesus, Brigid, Cailleach, Demeter, Hecate, Persephone, Sheela, and especially the Son of Wands and Priestess of Discs.

I owe the following cookbook luminaries a debt of gratitude for helping to shape my feelings about food and about good cooking.

Ginny Callan's delicious *Horn of the Moon Cookbook* first convinced me that I really could bake.

Mollie Katzen's sense of fun and her artist's sensibility have been a source of real delight.

Harriet Kofalk's *The Peaceful Cook* was a revelation for me: simple seasonal meals combined with mindfulness in the kitchen make so much nourishing sense.

Laurel Robertson is still my touchstone for simple and intelligent vegetarian cooking.

Anna Thomas's *Vegetarian Epicure* was one of the first vegetarian cookbooks I ever bought. It simply embodied luscious cooking for me, and showed me how to begin my sensual love affair with food.

Alice Waters' lovely *Fanny at Chez Panisse* is a feast for the eyes and the soul, as well as the palate. I find myself leafing through it whenever I need to feel that all is right with the world. And her *Chez Panisse Vegetables* features fresh seasonal recipes, inspiring in their simple elegance.

My most passionate thanks to my life-partner, Stuart Hannan, who spent countless hours creating the Hut, such a beautiful, dreamlike place for me to work. I am deeply grateful for everything he is, everything that he has given me, and for the life we have made together. And loving thanks to our son, Reid, who gamely tasted and commented on everything in this book. His suggestions were invaluable (when he said, of a very healthy dessert, "Mom, this tastes kinda like cardboard," the recipe was dropped. Health, schmealth).

My parents sent me elegant French kitchen gadgets and even my first food processor (until now, my kitchen has always been pretty low-tech); I so appreciate their encouragement.

And thanks to my enthusiastic (and patient) friends, who gave me cookbooks, showed me how to make new things, sent recipes, shared meals, made these foods for their families, and even came over to cook: Santha Cooke, Elizabeth Cunningham (for her Grace-ful poem and thoughtful comments: she is midwife to this project and so much more, my spirit-sister), Nadine Daugherty, Jeanne Englert, Elaine Fletcher, Cynthia Gayle, Fara Shaw Kelsey, Jessica Kemper, Pangea Jaeger, Donnalynne Lefever, Nina Lewis, Luis Perez, and Raven Wild. It was a great gift to birth this book surrounded by such loving support.

And my blessings on the people who made this a lovely book and a positive experience: Rowan Jacobsen, managing editor and wizard; my editor, Jon Graham, who is such a gentle pleasure to work with; Mary Elder Jacobsen, my wonderfully perceptive copyeditor; Virginia Scott, the book's gifted designer; Johanne Renbeck, for her magical, spirit-rich artwork; and Nancy Willard, whose beautiful poem at the beginning shines a little angel-light on everything that follows.

HOW TO STUFF A PEPPER

Now, said the cook, I will teach you
how to stuff a pepper with rice.

Take your pepper green, and gently,
for peppers are shy. No matter which side
you approach, it's always the backside.

Perched on green buttocks, the pepper sleeps.
In its silk tights, it dreams
of somersaults and parsley,
of the days when the sexes were one.

Slash open the sleeve
as if you were cutting a paper lantern,
and enter a moon, spilled like a melon,
a fever of pearls,
a conversation of glaciers.
It is a temple built to the worship
of morning light.

I have sat under the great globe
of seeds on the roof of that chamber,
too dazzled to gather the taste I came for.
I have taken the pepper in hand,
smooth and blind, a runt in the rich
evolution of roses and ferns.
You say I have not yet taught you

to stuff a pepper?
Cooking takes time.

Next time we'll consider the rice.

Nancy Willard

INTRODUCTION

This book is for all of us who would like cooking and eating to be more deeply soul-satisfying. If you have ever felt hungry after you've just eaten; if you long to recover the ancient sense that your hearth is sacred; if you want to feel more connected to the Earth and to your own inner Wild One; or if you simply need some inspiration in the kitchen, then *Cooking Like a Goddess* is for you.

Side by side with the recipes here are meditations, rituals, playful exercises—even decorating ideas—that deepen our relationship to food and to the Earth. We are all inextricably connected to our mother planet and to the food she gives us, but many of us have forgotten that the connection is a sacred one. When we remember this, then food may become the key to sacred experience. Our bodies will open the door and show us the way through. And the entire process can be great, nourishing fun.

So, welcome to the world of *Cooking Like a Goddess*, a world presided over by loving, seasonal goddesses who want nothing better than to share their gifts with us. Prepare to dance with them, to listen as they sing songs and tell stories—even to watch their films—as they show us how to fully appreciate each phase of the yearly cycle.

Together, we will explore the idea of cooking as a nourishing spiritual practice. This doesn't mean that we will need to spend more time cooking or that the meals we prepare will become more elaborate (in fact, they often become much simpler). Instead, exploring the sacredness of cooking means cooking with mindful awareness, with deeply felt pleasure and playful creativity, using foods that reflect the changing energies of the seasons, that are in harmony with the cycles of the Earth and those of your own body. This is truly cooking like a goddess.

The recipes in this book are all simple and comforting. Out of a mouth-watering multitude of possibilities, I chose these particular foods because they seem to typify each season, to be filled with those special flavors, colors, and textures. I relied upon my own tastes and intuition for inspiration, and I encourage you to do the same: if, for example, a particular food summons up springlike feelings in you but I didn't include it in the Spring section, by all means go ahead and cook it—with gusto—in Spring! This book is about trusting your longings and honoring who you are; the recipes are designed to allow plenty of creative individual variation.

It does our hearts good (both literally and figuratively, I think) to eat what Mahatma Ghandi called "innocent food," food that did not cause suffering to any living creature. The fact that there are many people starving on this planet of ours makes eating low on the food chain a humane priority. And there is a special sense of blessing, one that can be felt in every cell of our bodies, when we eat foods that come directly from our Mother Earth. And so, these recipes are vegetarian, not in any spirit of self-denial, but rather in the spirit of loving connection to the most vibrant and healthful energies of the Earth.

How we eat—our frame of mind and heart—may be just as important as what we eat. We can all name relatives or friends who drink like fish, smoke, eat terrible things, and are eighty years old and still going strong. Likewise, many of us are busy doing all the "right things"—fretting over proper food combinations, cutting out anything remotely "bad" or dangerous (no caffeine, no alcohol), agonizing over every gram of fat, and all the rest of it—and we're not exactly glowing with health.

Perhaps the key is to relax, connect with the Earth and the food it gives us, and live joyously. *Cooking Like a Goddess* is designed to help us live in a more joyful and connected way. And although there are no guarantees that joyful and connected living will prolong your life, it will certainly make life a pleasure while you live it.

One thing *Cooking Like a Goddess* is not designed to give you is guilt. Even though I love to cook, cooking is not my only spiritual practice: I don't spend all day, every day, in the kitchen fixing fancy meals for my family. I would often rather be making clay goddesses or reading or taking a walk in the woods or writing than cooking (in fact, I scorched one of the soups I was testing for this book because I got busy at the laptop and lost track of time). And I must confess that I take shortcuts when I need to; all-natural pilafs from a box, for instance, make a pretty consistent appearance on our table.

It may be that your life is too hectic to allow time for trying any of the meditations, rituals, or ideas. If that's so, don't worry: simply reading them will help. (Thousands of us curl up in bed with a good cookbook whenever we need comfort. Cookbooks often work even better than mysteries or escapist fantasies to give us what we need. And we don't necessarily cook the recipes we read about, either.)

The truth is, we are all very busy doing other things; food preparation isn't always at the top of our list of priorities. What really matters is not how much or how often we cook, but how deeply we pay attention when we do the cooking we do. Many of us are used to thinking that fixing a meal is something to rush through so we can get to the more important stuff. When we realize that cooking is itself an important, even a sacred act, perhaps we will no longer resent the time we spend in the kitchen. Perhaps we can be authentic, juicy, and deeply alive both in and out of the kitchen.

Cooking Like a Goddess invites us to interact with our food in playful and magical ways, to love our kitchens, our bodies, and our planet. When we welcome the goddesses of the seasons into our hearts, we will see that the magical world of this book is the real world that has surrounded and sustained us since the beginning of time. We will be priestesses in our kitchens, we will be cooking (and eating) like goddesses—and we will have come home.

GRACE

We say grace over food
forgetting that food
is grace the mystery
of the living goddess
in our mouths in our
bellies O bless bless
blessed be she yes
cook like a goddess
eat like a goddess
eat grace
may this book
be a blessing
eat.

Elizabeth Cunningham

PART ONE

Kitchen Magic

MAKING YOUR
KITCHEN A SACRED SPACE

If you have mixed feelings about your kitchen, you are not alone. Our attitudes toward kitchens and cooking are often weighted with lots of baggage, at least some of which is a legacy from our mothers, who often had pretty mixed feelings themselves. For many of our mothers, boxed and frozen foods were the saviors that liberated them from domestic tyranny, bought them a little free time; we may have grown up never knowing that food could taste alive. Others had moms who liked to do things the traditional way. Those meals probably tasted great, but we may have been thinking, as we chewed, "I am never going to spend five hours laboring over a meal that will get wolfed down in fifteen minutes. No such slavery for me, thank you!"

For some of us, even warm and cozy images of the kitchen are inextricably twined with images, just as strong, of patriarchal oppression: we know that there were generations of women who had no other arena for their abilities, no other outlet for their talents. With phrases like "barefoot, pregnant, and in the kitchen" echoing in our heads, kitchens can easily become symbols of frustration, of gifts denied. And those of us who truly love to cook may catch ourselves wondering, "Am I somehow unliberated? Is it politically incorrect to like hanging out in the kitchen? Should I be pacing a boardroom instead?"

Kitchens are often synonymous with some very complex issues. For instance, they automatically seem to bring up our deep-seated attitudes about sexual equality. Was your childhood kitchen solely your mother's domain? If it was, did your mom resent her kitchen responsibilities, or did she revel in her role as Kitchen Queen? Where did your dad fit in? Where did you? If you're in a relationship, how does your significant other fit into your kitchen scenario? Some of us have partners who never set foot in the kitchen. Others have partners who do all, or at least the majority, of the cooking.

What are the kitchen dynamics in your home? How do you feel about them?

The central truth—whether we're partnered or solo, on a high-powered career track, staying at home with our children, or somewhere in between—is that we all have to spend some time in the kitchen. We all have to eat. Some of us have to feed other people besides ourselves. And sadly, for many of us, kitchens are just rooms where we have to spend too much time, a place of tedious and soulless drudgery. It's no wonder that many of us feel tired, turned off, and bored as soon as we walk into them. Somehow, our culture has stolen the spirit from cooking, and from food. It is perhaps no coincidence that eating disorders are so prevalent: our very souls are hungry.

But what if we could restore a sense of magic, joy, and sacredness to the whole complex package of cooking and eating and kitchens? Imagine creating a kitchen that fills you with a sense of your own magical power—whether you spend three minutes a day cooking in it, or three hours. Imagine finding a way home to your ancient birthright of soul-nourishment and deep pleasure in food. Imagine cooking like a goddess.

This chapter offers a lively and empowering antidote to the cultural deadness surrounding kitchens, cooking, and food. In it, we are invited to create kitchens that are vivid expressions of our wild spirits, that resonate with our inner selves—kitchens where we can begin to feel deeply at home. By restoring a sense of the sacred to cooking and eating, we nourish our deep inner hunger, a hunger for connectedness and meaning. We can begin to create a concept of sacredness that embraces the everyday, that includes the playful and the spontaneous in its expression.

For all of us with mixed and complex feelings about kitchens and food, it can help to know that there is a newly rediscovered tradition, often called the Goddess Way, where food is considered holy, the body of our sacred Mother Earth, a loving gift to her children. Our culture may have forgotten, but our ancestors knew it; indigenous people have always known it. It is an Earth-centered way, meaning that it is grounded in loving respect for the planet. It is an ancient way, but it is reemerging today to remind us of our ancient Goddess heritage. According to the Goddess Way, food can be our spiritual guide, a guide that leads us to direct experience of the numinous, the Divine. Food is sacred. Our kitchens can be sacred, too.

Our culture considers cooking a chore; we are encouraged to get it over with as quickly as possible. But it may help us to remember that cooking was once a magical act. Cooks were priestesses who wielded the power of fire, transforming raw ingredients into nourishment for themselves and their families. The act of cooking linked women with the Goddess, the Great Nurturer. Now we can reclaim our power and joy in cooking, not because it is the only thing we are allowed to do, but because it is a sacred act and we are just the sacred folks to do it. We can reclaim the importance of the things women have always done—caretaking, teaching, relating, creating, mothering—because they have kept humanity alive despite our culture's message that only warfare, gaining power over others, consumerism, and competition are important.

Our culture may have taught us that we are widely separated by our differences—racial, religious, sexual, economic. But the need for food gives us all a common bond. And the fact that we are all inhabitants of this planet gives us another. Many of us are busy reenvisioning and remaking our culture in a healthier, more life-affirming mold. We want to imagine a culture where all of us are empowered to nurture each other, and ourselves. It can all start in the kitchen.

The following sections offer ideas for making your kitchen a place where magic can happen, a place that feels deeply right to you, an evocation of your unique and powerful spirit. Now, at this point, many of you may be thinking, "Look, I hardly have the time or energy to throw a frozen burrito in the microwave. Now I'm supposed to redecorate my kitchen? Are you kidding??"

The good news is, making your kitchen sacred is a process. Take it at the pace that feels right to you. Do only the things that feel fun. And use these ideas as inspiration for your own flights of spirit-fancy—there aren't any rules here except to follow your inclinations, listen to your heart. The great thing is, the more you make time to do, the more energy you'll have. Part of our deep spiritual exhaustion stems from the hours and hours we spend doing things that don't feed our spirits. Playing with magic in the kitchen will nourish and revive you.

Our ancestors knew the pleasure of being firmly rooted, in their kitchens, in their magic. Sadly, our culture is a rootless one. As my friend, novelist Elizabeth Cunningham says, most of us are walking around like cut flowers. Here, then, are some ideas and inspirations for putting down roots in the kitchen, making it a place where your goddess-self will feel deeply and joyously at home.

PUTTING DOWN ROOTS

The secret to making our kitchens sacred places is to connect: connect with inner self, connect with Deeper Power, connect with the living energies of the foods we cook. It is through the act of connection that we put down spirit-roots that draw up nourishment from the deep place to feed our hungry souls. And our greatest allies when it comes to this process of connecting and putting down roots are our senses.

Many of us have been taught that our bodies are lowly, even shameful, certainly inferior to the white light of Spirit. Our senses are not to be trusted, only our minds. Now many of us are realizing that this may not be the healthiest attitude to take. The ancient Goddess Way teaches us that our bodies are wise beyond our imagining; they give us cues to communicate their wisdom. Our bodies are, in fact, sacred and should be treated as sacred. Is it any wonder that the kitchen, so clearly tied to the needs of the body, should have been considered a lowly and inferior place for so long?

As we reclaim the sanctity of the body, we reclaim the sacredness of the kitchen. Trusting our senses is a first step. Our bodies need to be not only at ease, but pleased in the kitchen. We can't put down roots if the very sight, feel, and smell of the place makes us tense and unhappy. So, first we need to take a good look at the materials that were used to make our kitchens. Natural ones—wood, tile, brick—seem to encourage rooting, but materials that were man-made do not.

So, what do you do if yours is an artificial kitchen? Do you have to rip everything out and replace it with natural pine and earthy tile? Fortunately, no (unless you've just been searching for a project that would take lots of money and time). Instead, you could do what a friend did when she moved into her new home and was confronted with the Kitchen from the Chemical Lab: she put rag rugs over the linoleum, painted spirals and suns on the Formica cabinets, and replaced the Formica-topped built-in table with an old pine one. If you can't renovate, redecorate! Hopefully, the surfaces you see and touch most often will end up being pleasing to you.

CLEANING

A tidy kitchen is certainly not a prerequisite for sacred cooking—our inner Wild One has absolutely nothing against an exuberant mess. But a kitchen that smells weird or feels nasty can make your spirit cringe.

If you've been putting off the odious task of cleaning, you can make the process a more spirit-connected one in several ways:

1. Sing a special song as you clean. If you know a goddess song, great. If not, make something up. Repeating even the simplest of tunes (with or without rhyming words) can help you to relax, open, deepen. You don't have to sound like a "professional"—don't judge yourself, just have fun with it.

2. Clean barefoot. (Or naked.) This changes one's perspective, somehow. As you work, visualize rootlets growing from the soles of your feet, going down through your (clean) floor into the earth.

3. Make yourself a Cleaner's Crown out of ribbon or paper or ivy or anything that strikes your fancy. After all, you deserve a crown for all the work you do. Make up a

silly name for yourself. If you're a warrior-type, you could be Spic n' Spanna, Fighter of Grime; make up stories about your battles and adventures. Or become Our Lady of Perpetual Mopping; see yourself as a healer and soother, a sort of Mother Theresa of the kitchen. Your crown would be more of a halo. Maybe you'd be happy as the Wise One of the Woods, wreathed with wild grapevine, breasts painted with magical symbols (real or imagined). Find a character that suits you.

4. Nothing discourages rooting like toxic and carcinogenic chemicals. If your cleaning products are filled with them, you can bet your inner self knows it—and it probably isn't happy. Check out the many wonderful books available today that tell how to make safe, effective household cleaners from simple and natural ingredients (see the Suggested Reading section for titles). Or take a trip to your nearest natural foods store and try some of the earth-friendly products you'll find there. You'll be doing yourself, your family, and the environment a favor—and you'll feel a healthy difference in your kitchen. Imagine wiping away the grease with a liquid made of deliciously scented citrus peels instead of harsh chemicals. Or scouring the sink with fresh lemon and baking soda rather than something that smells like a public swimming pool. What you choose to use can really make a difference: try paper towels made from non-chlorine-bleached recycled paper, or switch to washable cloths. When you grocery-shop, bring along a string bag, or a sturdy canvas one. Compost your kitchen scraps, rather than just throwing them away. Actually, composting can become a satisfying part of our daily spiritual practice. Here is a Compost Prayer from my friend Pangea. She repeats it every time she takes the kitchen scrap crock outside to empty it onto her compost heap:

From the earth you came—
Your seed did grow,
Nourishing all of me, body and soul,

An eternal cycle,
A graceful flow—
And now, back into the earth you go.
Blessed be, Mother Earth. Thank you.

Even small, everyday choices like these can show that we care about the planet. After all, when we put down roots, we want the earth we root in to be healthy and safe.

5. Add a strong herbal tea to your cleaning water. The sweet scent and good vibes will go a long way toward making your kitchen feel connected to Deep Power. Just boil a couple of cups of water and throw in a handful of herbs, steep for several minutes, and then strain the tea into your cleaning bucket.

Here are some traditional herb correspondences. Choose one or more according to your desire. We don't usually think of things like sea salt or basil or apples as magical, but our ancestors knew they were. It is a wonderful affirmation of the magic in the ordinary to use kitchen-cupboard ingredients consciously in this way.

angelica—blessings, protection, purification. Those of you who are fascinated by angels will like this one: think of it as inviting angels into your home.

apples—food of the Goddess, love. Simply add a few pieces of fresh or dried apple to your boiling water (but not too much, or you'll end up with a sticky kitchen).

basil—love, fidelity, wealth, protection. A nice all-purpose herb with a luscious summery scent reminiscent of mouth-watering pesto.

chamomile—serenity and calm, purification. Smells like a blend of apples and new-mown hay. While you're at it, make yourself a cup to drink after you've finished cleaning; it's very relaxing.

cinnamon—happy home, safety, healing, protection. The primal home-and-hearth spice. Use pieces of cinnamon stick for your brew (the powdered kind will turn into a gelatinous glop in the bowl).

clove—purification, promotes love and spirituality. Try it with cinnamon—delicious!

eucalyptus—health, protection. Slightly medicinal, but warm and fresh.

evergreen—health, purification, vitality. Different types have different scents, so experiment. If you have pine, cedar, or juniper growing nearby, a few sprigs placed in boiling water will add green freshness to the brew.

fennel—protection, healing. Its licorice scent has a childlike quality that's very appealing.

lavender—love, friendship, peace, happiness, protection. Such a sweet, relaxing, and calm-inducing scent! Antidepressant.

lemon peel (fresh or dried)—purification. It's no accident that so many cleaning products are lemon-scented: lemon smells fresh and uplifting. Cleanses away negativity.

marjoram—love, protection. Another antidepressant. Some of us sprinkle a little of this dried herb in the corners of every room in the house (why stop with the kitchen?) to promote love and safety.

peppermint—purification, healing, soothing. A wonderfully relaxing and refreshing scent.

rosemary—cleansing, protection, clears negativity, encourages clear thinking. You may find that a rosemary-scented kitchen is one where you have to consult the recipe less often because you'll find yourself remembering what it says!

sage—purification, wisdom (no coincidence that the word for *wise one* is the same as the herb's name). A traditional ingredient of many Native American smudge-bundles, a strong sage tea will make your kitchen feel safe and cleared of negativity.

St. Joan's (or John's) Wort—health, happiness, love, protection. An all-purpose herb. It doesn't really have a scent, but a few drops of tincture—or a few blossoms strewn in the wash-water—give many benefits. Consult a good weed-identification book to see if there is any growing near you, or see Supplies to order the tincture.

sea salt—traditional for purification and protection. If you've been feeling vulnerable or weird and you only have time to add one ingredient to your water, this could be it.

vanilla—love, happiness. A piece of the bean or a few drops of extract will make your kitchen smell and feel delicious.

If you're stressed for time or low on ingredients, try the herbal tea bag shortcut: there are many varieties available at the supermarket with nice combinations of ingredients already premixed for you. For instance, Celestial Seasonings makes a fragrant cinnamon-apple blend, perfect for happy-home and goddess-centered energies. If it's serenity in the kitchen that you want, try one of the many stress-reducing or relaxing blends available. Just boil a few cups of water, add a couple of bags, steep, and strain as usual.

Or you could use a few drops of essential oil instead of either tea bags or herbs. Consult a good book on aromatherapy to see which scents would be most beneficial for you and your family.

6. After you have vanquished the worst of the grime, clear the atmosphere by lighting a sweetgrass braid or sage-based smudge bundle and walk around the room, letting the smoke waft into every corner (let some smoke waft into the cupboards, too). Or light a stick or cone of your favorite incense. You want your kitchen to smell good to your inner self.

7. You may surprise yourself and really get into the cleaning process. If you do (and if you have some more time), you may enjoy clearing out and beautifully organizing your cupboards. Virgo-type friends report that every time they open a tidied cupboard, the sight of neatly arranged cans and jars—or cups and plates—gives them a rush of serenity and well-being. Even non-Virgos can enjoy this.

8. Take some special time in your now-clean kitchen, simply being, doing nothing. You will be amazed at how soothing this can be. Make yourself a cup of tea and just sit and drink it. Slowly. Quietly. Listen to the hum of your refrigerator. Smell the incense or smudge or herbs that you used. Feel the shape of the chair under your seat, the firmness of the floor under your feet. You are enspiriting your kitchen—now you can allow yourself to feel welcomed by that spirit, which you are helping to create.

THE POWER PLACE

One of the most important first steps in making your kitchen sacred is to create a place of nurturance for yourself there. We deserve to have a special spot where we can relax, close our eyes and meditate, daydream, or simply think about food in peace. Tuning in to your inner self—and feeling empowered—are more difficult when your muscles are tensed. You are the goddess of your kitchen: you deserve to be comfortable.

All you really need is a special, cozy chair—one that everyone in your home recognizes as yours. Every time you sit in it, you will remember that you are doing sacred work when you cook, and you will remember that comfort was once the special gift of the kitchen.

Even though many of our modern kitchens are sleek, almost chilly places, something in our bones remembers when kitchens were snug. Deep inside us, we remember the magical glow from a cave-fire: outside its bright circle of protection were all our fears—hungry wild beasts, killing cold, shapeless terrors that waited in the dark. But inside the golden circle we were safe. Kitchens—places where the hearth-fires burn—mean safety, warmth, peace. For centuries, the kitchen was virtually the only comfortable room in the house. Before central heating, its roaring fires and ovens kept out the chill when the world was blanketed with snow. The kitchen became a natural gathering place, with special seats built near the fireplace where one could rest and be at ease, warm, and comfortable.

Hold that image of warmth and comfort in your mind while you look around your kitchen. Is the seating soft and inviting? Is there any seating at all? If you live in a tiny city apartment, you may not even have room for a chair. In this case, you can design a movable cushioned space for yourself on the floor: you can move the cushion when you need to open the oven door.

If you do have space for a table and chairs, really notice how they feel. Kitchen chairs are often hard and bumpy. If your chair makes your seat and spirit sore, consider haunting yard sales and thrift shops until you find a rounder, softer, or more cushioned alternative. An acquaintance flouted convention recently and bought herself a lush, forties-style brocaded armchair from the Salvation Army for her kitchen corner. Now she can curl up and read cookbooks (or murder mysteries) lapped in luxury. She reports that it has changed the way she feels about her kitchen forever. Having a place to plop down and relax while the stew is bubbling or the bread is baking feels very soothing to the soul.

We create inviting kitchens, not only for ourselves, but for our families. Most of us have a real longing to share our emerging sense of deep nourishment with the people we love. But, even though we want to share our kitchens with loved ones, it is important for us to stake out this special chair or spot for ourselves alone. Accessing our inner power is much easier when we have a place from which to access it. A Power Place becomes an important part of our conscious effort to reclaim the role of Kitchen Priestess, freeing ourselves from the martyrdom and domestic slavery so long associated with kitchen work. And children who see their parent consciously modeling this claiming of kitchen power will have an easier time growing into their own some day.

So, claim your spot, and fill your kitchen with textures and colors that make you feel nourished and safe. When we make the kitchen a serene and comfortable place, we create a heart of safety in a very unsafe world. It is what women have done for eons: made nests of nurturance and peace for their families. We need those nests now more than ever.

CONVENIENCE

Most of us organize our kitchens the way our mothers organized theirs: after all, it's what we grew up with, what we're used to. But it is often worth some time and thought to see if a few changes would make your kitchen feel more like you, more appropriate for who you are. Why not put your boxes of tea bags in the same cabinet as the mugs and cups? Then you'd only have to open one door to make a cup of tea. Why not devote an entire cupboard to herbs and spices if you want to? Or, if you paint, why not set aside a shelf for your supplies? Or clear a space on the table for the laptop, if you're a writer? It's wonderfully empowering to free ourselves from compartmentalized thinking and living. Ask yourself, "Why not?" if you want to do something a little different. There's no reason why we can't make room in the kitchen for the activities we love most deeply. Making our lives a seamless whole is a task fit for a goddess.

ALLIES IN THE KITCHEN

Most of us use gadgets, utensils, and appliances when we cook. There are elaborate electronic ones, ranging from fancy food processors, cappuccino machines, dishwashers, microwaves, and breadmakers to the more ubiquitous refrigerators and blenders. Even the low-tech cook usually has a toaster or an electric hand-held beater. Not everybody has egg separators or apple corers, but we all use knives, spatulas, and spoons. And a kitchen isn't a kitchen without an oven and a stove.

Most of us make use of these kitchen allies every day—and a sudden power failure has shown more than a few of us how dependent on the electric ones we are. But for many of us, appliances can feel a little alien. We may find ourselves thinking, "I don't know how the heck it works, so it must be dangerous." And even the most technologically dauntless among us has been known to curse a faulty appliance when things go wrong. When we're not secretly fearing or actively despising our appliances, we remain somehow aloof and detached from them—after all, they're just hunks of metal and plastic from the store. But this distancing is not conducive to rooting. Our ancestors made all of their kitchen utensils lovingly by hand: their tools were rich with spirit-value. So how can we create an aura of warmth and friendliness around the tools we use? The answer is by personalizing them.

Try imagining our appliances as helpful genies who gladly share space in our kitchens in order to do our bidding—the bidding of the Kitchen Priestess. Take some time to really look at them, their colors, their shapes. By simply observing them, we can discover (or invent) their personalities. A battered old automatic dishwasher, for instance, could be seen as a rounded, genial type, dowdy but capable—and very different from the assertive, breezy new toaster with its slick, shiny finish. We may choose to honor these newly discovered personalities by naming our appliances, just as many of us name our cars. ("Hold on, Dante's preheated, I've got to put the muffins in"; "We'll have clean glasses in a minute, Ethel's nearly finished her dry cycle"; "Could you put the leftovers in the Igloo?")

If that's just not your style, you could try a different approach, which involves making your own personal and individual mark on the tools you use. Try decorating your appliances and utensils, either subtly or not so subtly, depending on your preference. Children's stickers or lick-and-stick stamps are quick ways to do this; the more artistically inclined may want to hand-paint or stencil something personally significant—a totem animal, a favorite flower or fruit, a special symbol. The handles of your wooden tools may be carved; plastic ones may be painted.

Touching a drop of your favorite essential oil to your major appliances is another way to mark them, much as a cat rubs its chin glands on things to show territory or special preference. Or, if you feel your inner Wild One stirring, you could use your own saliva to celebrate your bond with your kitchen allies!

The simple act of consciously choosing to buy only things that are pleasing to your eye and to your touch is another way to give spirit to your utensils: the antique eggbeater that holds a mysterious appeal for you will make the act of whipping cream with it a real pleasure, even though it takes longer than with a fancy electric gadget. You may also notice that kitchen gifts from special friends make you feel warm and happy every time you take one out of the drawer.

Certainly, the plates and bowls, cups, glasses, and eating utensils you use should be pleasing to you. If they're not, consider having a swap with friends: you may have just what the other wants or needs. If you have pottery skills and access to clay and a kiln, you could make a simple set of dinnerware yourself, as one friend's husband did. Or you could collect plates and bowls hand-thrown by your favorite potter, piece by piece, as you can afford them. Thrift shops and yard sales often yield magical treasures, like the tiny brass teaspoons, each with a different mythical beast on the handle, that were a garage-sale gift from my partner, or my favorite Staffordshire plate painted with autumnal grapes and roses, bought for a dollar at the Salvation Army.

But the simplest method of connecting with the things in your kitchen involves nothing more complicated than using those tools with consciousness. Become aware of their smoothness, their shape, the way they move or work, the noises they make. Hum along with your dishwasher, or hold your hands next to a hot oven and feel the power of its flame. When you push a button or pick a setting, explore your own goddess-power to choose, to do, to make.

CREATIVITY

Each of the four seasonal sections coming up includes many ideas for decorating your kitchen creatively and in harmony with the Earth. The most important thing will be to trust your sense of what is *right for you*.

Part of owning our goddess-power is throwing out the "shoulds" and "should nots" around our kitchens. Who says we shouldn't hang a phalanx of winged goddesses over the sink? Who says we shouldn't hand-paint bright suns and flowers on the backsplash behind the countertops, or on the fridge if we want to? Who says we have to paint anything at all if we really like things bare? It's your kitchen. (If you are a renter with a longing for painted decoration and the owner disapproves, you could explore the ways in which double-stick tape can be used to apply unusual shapes and colors to your appliances and cupboards—temporarily.)

This book is based on creativity: trusting inner self, really taking time to savor and experience food, allowing our inclinations and the nature of the ingredients themselves to determine what we cook. When our kitchen becomes the reflection of a creative relationship with inner self, we affirm creativity in every aspect of our lives.

COMMUNITY

Kitchens can be the perfect place to party. Many of us have often noted that the kitchen is where guests tend to congregate anyway, whether you want them to or not. You may want to throw a kitchen-warming party in honor of your newly consecrated cooking space: invite your closest friends and family for a potluck, or, better yet, have a Community Cook, to which everybody brings raw ingredients. Cooking them becomes a group effort (depending on the size of your kitchen and the amount of wine consumed, this can be a fairly hilarious process).

When we invite the people we love to celebrate our sacred kitchen with us, we set the seal of that love on our efforts, and we invest the room with happy memories and good energy. And we also create a vital sense of community based on the values of the sacred kitchen. What a lovely, lively way to spread the word!

THE KITCHEN ALTAR

Many cultures still make a place in their kitchens to honor Greater Power. We can, too. A kitchen altar makes a vital, visual connection between you and your cooking activities and this power, whatever you conceive it to be. If the oven and stove, as modern equivalents of the hearth-fire, are the heart of the house, this altar will be the soul. Every time you see it, you will be reminded that what you do is vitally important. It will remind you that your kitchen is a sacred place. It will help you remember that your ability to nourish yourself and your loved ones connects you with the Great Mother, the nourisher, the spirit of loving and compassionate care.

And the kitchen altar is meant to be a joyous and playful expression of your wild spirit: creating it is great fun! Whenever we consciously allow inner self to come out and play, a deep satisfaction results from feeding our spirits, nurturing our souls. While your altar will be unique because each one of us is so different, it is also comforting to know that it connects us to many, many other people with unique altars of their own.

Here, then, are some guidelines to help you get started. You could also check out some books from your local library or bookstore—pictures of altars from different countries will be sure to inspire you (see Russia's gilded kitchen icons, the terra-cotta niches of Mexico, or any of the powerful elemental altars found in many African countries). Search out the cultures that most closely match your own heritage, if you like. Or wing it and invent your own.

KITCHEN GODDESSES

It is very ancient and powerful magic to have a goddess figure in your home. Some of the earliest human artifacts ever discovered include many domestic goddess statues. When we create an altar and house a goddess there, we are making a satisfying link with our earliest ancestors. Many of us have found that having a female figure in this place of honor just feels deeply right. (It's difficult to even picture any of the great male religious figures bent over a cooking pot, stirring away.) And, although goddess worship was officially squelched for centuries, scores of kitchen madonnas from cultures around the globe prove you just can't keep a good goddess down.

Today, we can find or create special kitchen goddesses to be the focus for our altars. In fact, a good first step in creating your altar is choosing the goddess you wish to honor with it. Your kitchen altar becomes this deity's home, as well as a place to honor who *you* are and what *you* do.

When you make a kitchen altar, you begin a special, personal, and very intimate relationship with your kitchen goddess. In some ways, the two of you will echo each other: it is important to choose a goddess who embodies traits and values that you desire or with whom you can identify. There are several books in the Suggested Reading section that will help you pick one that is right for you. Or you could make one up, invent or recreate a goddess especially for your kitchen.

Once you've decided on your goddess, you may purchase one—there are several wonderful sources for reproductions of ancient figures (see Supplies)—or you can make your own with clay or Sculpey or papier-mâché, or improvise something magical with twigs, weeds, or fabric. Remember, goddesses are easy and fun to make.

If three-dimensional figures aren't your style (or you aren't able to find one that you like), try cutting out a photo or painting and gluing it onto cardboard. You can create a textured border around this flat surface with glue and trim, or with tendrils of ivy or some other potted house plant.

The expression on your goddess's face is very important: you'll find that it can affect your cooking mood. A picture of mild-faced Hestia, eyes peacefully focused on the hearth-fire, will give you one feeling while Kali, with her necklace of skulls, fierce scowl, and tongue hanging out, will give you quite another. And there is certainly no law against having more than one kitchen goddess. They can be rotated to suit the season or your mood; you could let them take turns vacationing, soaking up some sun in the backyard, letting someone else take her turn on the altar.

And we certainly don't need to exclude males here. One friend is perfectly happy with her (male) kitchen dragon, while another tells me that her kitchen goddess has a consort from Trinidad—"And who knows what they get up to when we're not looking!" If you want to have a male kitchen deity, great! (Ironically, with all of my own personal emphasis on the Goddess, it was a male—the Son of Wands from the *Motherpeace Tarot* deck—who appeared in a Tarot session and encouraged me to continue this cookbook project.)

PLACEMENT

Your kitchen altar can be almost anywhere in the room—on a countertop, on top of a cupboard or the fridge, on the table. You'll just want to be sure that it won't get bumped or broken in the midst of your cooking activities (but if it gets a little spattered with cooking juices, it shouldn't hurt). Find a spot near the stove or oven, if possible. Many kitchen goddesses are pretty hot and fiery, and they love to be right where the action is (not only can they take the proverbial heat in the kitchen, they thrive on it).

If you feel like doing a little minor renovation, you could hollow out a niche in a kitchen wall to house your altar. Or you can improvise a setting for your altar with a special box—ransack the attic or check out yard sales to find the perfect one. Your altar can be set inside or on top of it. Or you could take a trip to the nearest craft shop; they often sell lovely wild-looking twiggy birdhouses that make terrific kitchen altars.

The shape of your altar, as well as the decorations you choose for it, will depend in large measure on not only your taste, but on the taste of your goddess (a primitive terra-cotta bird-headed goddess would probably feel more at home in one of the aforementioned wild, twiggy nests than in a columned and frescoed temple). If you decide on an actual historical goddess, you may want to read up on her to find out what she'd like; make sure your tastes are compatible.

HONORING WHO YOU ARE

One of the most important functions of your kitchen altar is to remind you of your intimate connection with Deeper Power. It also celebrates the unique gifts and talents you bring to the kitchen—and to the world—as a human representative of nurturing goddess-energy. What small objects could you include on the altar to express who you are? A painter friend did a small still-life oil painting of her favorite foods for her altar. An avid needlewoman cross-stitched a very female-looking background for hers (she says she was inspired by Judy Chicago's *The Dinner Party*). An attorney found a small metal scale, symbol of justice, to dangle from the hand of her Kitchen Athena, and a potter threw a tiny spiral-painted pot to rest at her clay goddess's feet. Writer-friends have made books from paper, lace, or cornhusks to place on their altars; a teacher places a piece of chalk in her Hestia's hand; and a marathon runner includes a tiny pair of track shoes from her daughter's cast-off doll wardrobe.

If you have a special love for any particular animal, you can find or make a small one to share the altar space with your goddess. Collectors may want to find a spot for an item from their button or stamp or kitchen magnet collections. Find ways to share your talents and enthusiasms via the altar.

You could also create a special ancestor feast to remind you of your unique place in the unbroken chain of life.

ANCESTOR FEASTS

Most of us have fond food-based memories of a grandparent or other close relative. What did they like to cook? Were there any special foods they made just for you? My grandmother knew how much I loved her cornbread, which she baked in a special tin shaped like little ears of corn; she sent boxes of these cornsticks to me whenever she could. I can never get mine to taste the same, but it is a mark of my respect for her— a way of honoring who she was—to bake them in her memory.

Who would you like to honor in this way? If not a specific relative, think about the ancestors in your past. Where did they live? What foods did they eat? In a very real way, you can bring alive your blood-link to these people by fixing foods that are connected with them and sharing the meal with your family. Your ancestors are part of who you are; you are the continuation of their line. If you have children, you can teach them how they fit into this unbroken line of life by involving them in these special ancestor feasts. Older children might want to research the foods and customs specific to the countries that birthed your relations. Everyone can get involved in selecting and preparing the food. You may want to take a few moments before the meal to light a candle in tribute and say a few words about your own special, unique heritage. It is part of what has made you the goddess that you are. Place a bit of your special food on your altar to honor your roots.

DECORATION

While the choices for altar decoration are virtually limitless, here are a few basics to get you started.

> **candles:** Candles become the visible reminder of the hearth-flame. Small tea-lights in aluminum cups work very well, and they often burn for just the amount of time it takes to plan, prepare, cook, and eat a meal. Or you could

use votives (many of them have food-related fragrances: apple-cinnamon, honeydew, pumpkin-pie spice, vanilla) or regular tapers or pillar candles. The simple act of lighting your altar candle before you start your meal preparation can make a profound difference in the way you feel about cooking. Just be sure not to leave it burning unattended, or you may end up getting a visit from the fire department.

food: Our distant ancestors left bits of their meals at the feet of the hearth goddess. It can be soul-satisfying for us to do this, as well. Perishable items will need to be removed and replaced regularly. Those of us who tend to be a little lax about getting rid of the food before it gets nasty can stick to dried seeds, herbs, nuts, Native American corn—anything that won't spoil.

natural objects: When we include something from nature on the altar, especially something that is relatively unchanging like a special rock or crystal, we are reminded of how ancient the planet is, and how brief has been the span of human life upon it. It's good to root our altars in the ancientness of Earth.

seasonal reminders: The four seasonal sections coming up will give suggestions for seasonal goodies that you can rotate according to the time of year: seeds for late Summer, a small squash for harvest time, evergreen sprigs for midwinter, sprouts for early Spring. What is in season now? Pay real attention when you explore farmer's markets, or take a walk outdoors and notice what the green things are doing. The world is filled with incredible bounty and richness. The altar is a perfect place to celebrate this delightful truth.

utensils: It can be fun to honor the utensils with which we cook. Dollhouses often yield beautiful miniature utensils that fit well on kitchen altars, or you can follow the lead of artist Tasha Tudor and make them yourself out of various materials: her handmade Victorian dollhouse features a fully equipped kitchen of her own creation. Small wooden cooking spoons are a favorite, but you may prefer a miniature eggbeater, a minute mortar and pestle, or a teensy food processor.

incense and burner: Most of us don't burn incense before we begin preparing a meal, because we don't want to mask all the wonderful cooking aromas. But lighting a special stick or cone of incense is a satisfying way to bring closure to the meal. (Many of us also find that it helps the dishwasher to get into the proper frame of mind.)

reminders of loved ones: It can be a special act of love to include small photos or mementos for each family member or friend whom we'll be feeding. When we bring visible reminders of our tenderness into the kitchen, it helps us to cook with a joyous, open heart.

CONSECRATION

An important part of creating your altar is taking a few moments to bless or consecrate it. How you do this is up to you. You could simply take a deep breath, close your eyes, open them again, look all around your kitchen, and exhale. You could say a few words: "This kitchen is now a sacred place," or "May the food that is cooked in this sacred kitchen feed us deeply." You may choose to do something more elaborate, sprinkling the altar with salt and water, smudging it with incense or a smudge stick, reading a passage from a poem or other work that has meaning to you. The important thing is for you to find your own way to say, "Here it is, I did this," to your inner self, and to the Deeper Power.

THE KITCHEN GODDESS FEAST

Another way to celebrate the emergence of your kitchen as a magical and holy place is to throw a Kitchen Goddess Feast. What would your kitchen goddess like to eat? What region or culture does your goddess evoke? Think of ways to honor her with food. Athena or Artemis may enjoy Greek-style grape leaves stuffed with rice and nuts and feta cheese. Irish Brigid might be partial to oatcakes or potatoes and cabbage. Then again, your goddess may be heartily sick of the same old thing: you could expand her food horizons and offer her something wildly different from her usual fare. Invite your friends—you could take turns hosting Kitchen Goddess Dinners. Wear costumes and play special music, if you like. The Goddess loves a good time.

Now that your kitchen is bubbling with divine female energy, ready for some soul-nourishing cooking to happen, we can turn our attention to our own magical adornment.

MAKING A KITCHEN GODDESS APRON

"Apron" is a word loaded with associations. How many of us remember the fifties, and those sitcoms where every woman was a wife, and every wife wore an apron (along with a saintly smile)? Perhaps it's time to reclaim our Right of the Apron. Nobody relishes the idea of getting cooking gunk all over her clothes; aprons are practical. And there are certainly thousands upon thousands of styles and patterns to choose from out there, many of which don't even make us look like Donna Reed—or the Beaver's mother.

But what if we could make or decorate an apron that we donned like a high priestess's robe, an apron that expressed something essential about ourselves and made a clear visual statement about our magical cooking power? It's not hard to create or decorate a special apron. And it's not an endless project; you only take the time you have. The process is a lot of fun, and when it's done, every time you put on your personal apron you will be reminding yourself (and anybody who sees you) that you are a kitchen goddess. You may find that apron-decorating quickly becomes a party: get some friends together, pool your resources, and encourage and empower each other!

Here's how to get started. First, choose a basic apron style.

Some people favor from-the-waist-down aprons. Some like an apron with a bib. Others may opt for a full-body model that goes over the head and ties at the waist. Which style suits you?

Most of us don't have the time to machine-sew (let alone hand-sew) much of anything. But if you do, more power to you—you can imbue your apron with lots of personal energy and power with every stitch. Buy a pattern and sew your own. Or you may feel like trying your hand at clothing design: your apron could be patterned after a Kate Greenaway smock, or a Victorian pinafore, or a Medieval tabard. Sci-fi buffs could go for a futuristic look, or you could honor our primitive forebears by making a fake animal-skin tied on one shoulder. Look at costume history books, or historical paintings. Feel free to be as silly or serious as you like.

You may need more than one apron to suit your different moods. One friend has a fairly plain one for everyday, and a *Little House on the Prairie* kind of thing with hand-smocking and flounces for those days when she feels the blood of her pioneer ancestors stirring in her veins, and is moved to gather wild greens for cooking, or to make corn pone, or biscuits. She wears bare feet with this apron.

APRON DECORATION

For the majority of us who just don't have the time to make our own, here is a time-saving alternative that produces wonderfully satisfying results. Buy yourself a plain, off-white canvas or muslin apron—you'll find them in natural clothing or earth-friendly products catalogs, or at your local hardware or kitchenware store. Then, using dye or fabric paint (or hand-embroidery or appliqué), color and decorate it as your spirit desires.

Here are some ideas, from the conservative to the outrageous. Use them as springboards for your own inspiration.

1. Find a symbol or shape that is meaningful to you and incorporate it: spirals, triangles, circles, eyes, pomegranates, different animals, fruits or vegetables, wheatsheaves, flowers, weeds—there are no limits to the possibilities. What matters is for the symbol to feel important to you. You could do a border of your symbols around the bottom of your apron, or place a large one on the chest (or wherever). You can achieve professional-looking results in no time with rubber stamps—look in your local gift or craft shop for them (or try the magical goddessy ones from Kate Cartwright; see the Supplies section at the end of the book); or use stencils—your local bookstore probably carries the handsome Dover stencil books with designs that range from Ancient Egyptian to Art Nouveau.

2. Find a picture that feels special to you and paint a copy of it on your apron—or go to the mall and see if they can do a photo-transfer for you. Some copy shops can do this, too.

3. Do you have a personal affinity for any particular colors or fabrics? This is the place to use them. You can cut shapes out of fabric and fuse them to your apron with the iron-on webbing they sell in fabric stores. If you like to sew, consider making appliqué designs.

4. Hot-glue guns make it easy to apply trim—buttons, ribbon, braid, raffia—anything that feels fun and right to you. The final product won't be washable, but this work of magical art doesn't need to last forever. When it gets grubby, it's time to make a new one—you will have probably evolved some new symbols and colors by then, anyway. And you can recycle buttons or jewelry to use on your next creation!

5. You could glue or sew on earrings that have lost their mates, or pendants, or entire necklaces. One friend sewed a long Native American corn necklace around the neck of her apron. (You can make beautiful necklaces out of Native American corn.

For directions on making these and many other magical things, see *Celebrating the Great Mother: A Handbook of Earth-Honoring Ideas for Parents and Children*, which I coauthored with Maura D. Shaw.)

6. Those of us who love words could embroider or paint a few on our aprons. Once again, rubber stamps—with many styles available for the different letters of the alphabet—could make this process a quick one. Goddess names are good: see a book or two from the Suggested Reading section and pick a goddess that resonates with you. Your own name would be good, or the name of the persona you use when cleaning (see Cleaning, page 10). Any evocative word that has a special meaning for you will work—the watchwords in each seasonal section may give you some ideas.

7. Add wacky personal touches. A nearby friend has a Surprise Pocket on her apron, which she keeps filled with small treats for her children (the fee for a surprise is some help with a kitchen chore). If you enjoy choosing a Tarot card for the day, you could put a clear plastic window on the breast of your apron to display it. Rubber snakes, bats, and spiders are the decorations of choice for one Halloween-loving friend, while another added a pink curly tail to the rear of her smock-style apron.

Can you picture a bright yellow-gold apron with a huge tomato painted on it and the word *BOLD* or *WILD* or *JUICY* blazoned across the chest? Or an apron with a pomegranate on the bib, its seeds made of tiny hand-sewn garnet seeds, and goddess names in a border around the hem? Maybe you would make a tie-dyed apron with gold spirals and love beads (many of us remember the sixties with fond nostalgia), or one with graphics from a favorite T-shirt sewn over the bib, or another with appliquéd, stuffed vegetables and eggplant-colored rickrack zigzagging all over. You are the goddess of your hearth—what would this goddess like to wear? You have the power to create it.

And you can also create what you *need*. As my friend Rowan says, "Before I made my special Hestia apron, I really hated housecleaning—I thought it was the most dismal chore. But now, before I start, I sing this song that I made up and I put on my apron. It's changed everything. The fact is, my house may not be all that much cleaner, but I sure feel better about it! And that's what matters."

(Sing to the tune of "I'll Never Fall In Love Again")

What do you do when you just can't start?
You could put on the Apron of Hestia—
Gird your loins and then the resta ya!
I'll never hate to clean again.
I'll never hate to clean again.

FOR THE VERY BOLD

Food and sex are two basic pleasures that go very well together (see the infamous eating scene in the classic film *Tom Jones*, for example). There is no reason why your kitchen goddess apron can't be sensual or even erotic.

Feel like cooking something romantic, perhaps aphrodisiac, for your partner? Try wearing your apron and nothing but your apron. This sort of thing would work very well at Beltane, the May first celebration of sensuality and fertility.

You could put generous painted or appliquéd goddesslike breasts on your apron. (One friend drew different foods pouring from her apron-breasts like milk. What the heck!) Or, for the truly adventurous, paint a vulva in the appropriate spot—you could be the Sheela-na-gig of the kitchen. (Sheelas are wonderful goddesses who have been proudly displaying their vulvas for centuries, many of them in carvings on old Irish churches, of all places.) Find your own ways to be daring and risqué in the kitchen!

KITCHEN RITUALS

Some traditions teach that you should cook only if your heart is open and filled with joy. As one friend tersely put it, "Well, if I waited for that, my family would starve." The truth is, we can't always be in a great mood when we cook. But it is also true that, just as food is made not only of chemicals but of life-energy, so the food you cook is imbued with your own energy—the mood you're in, your state of mind and spirit. The greatest gift you can give yourself and anyone who eats your food is a few moments of time-out before you begin, time to relax, to breathe deeply and with attention, time to heal from the stresses of the day. Kitchen rituals are ways to help you do this. More than anything else, the creation and performance of simple kitchen rituals will help you to cook like a goddess.

A ritual is any action performed with intention. Although the word has come to mean elaborate, repetitive, and probably arcane rites, it really isn't so. Rituals are meant to alter our awareness, to bring us into a deeper mode of being or perceiving. Ritual activity before we cook will help us to approach cooking in a more mindful, sacred way. But this never needs to be a solemn thing (unless you'd like it to be), and certainly not a pretentious one. Your kitchen ritual may be nothing more complicated than taking a deep breath and lighting a candle before you begin to cook—but it still counts. And it still works.

Here are some possibilities, starting with my own personal favorite: the glass-of-wine ritual (some of us have been doing this one for years, we just didn't know it counted). Sit in your Power Place. Pour yourself (and a friend or partner, if available) a glass of wine. (If you are avoiding alcohol, a glass of some pure, fresh fruit juice will work just as well.) First, really notice the color. Hold it to the light and look through it, see how your kitchen looks from the other side. Now take a whiff and enjoy the pleasant muskiness or earthiness. Now sip it slowly, thoughtfully. Savor the complex flavors and scents. Is that a hint of black currant or myrrh? Is there an aftertaste of apples or spice? Imagine the ripe, smooth grapes and the lush vineyards that produced this wine. Outside it may be cold and drizzly, but the slopes where those grapes grew were sunny and warm. The fertile richness of earth, the powerful energy of the sun, are in this glass of wine. Give yourself fully to the experience of enjoying it. When it is gone, thank it.

One friend takes her favorite wooden spoon and taps on the countertop before she begins to cook, like a conductor before a concert, rapping on the podium for the orchestra's attention. Another uses her precooking hand-washing as a part of her spiritual practice: as she soaps her hands, she does a check-in of her present condition, emotional, mental, and physical, "Today, I'm feeling irritable and stressed. I didn't get enough sleep because the dog threw up on the bed at 3:00 A.M. I got caught in traffic, and I didn't have time to go to the farmer's market, so we have to eat whatever's in the fridge." Then, as she rinses, she says, "That's the way it is. But now my hands are clean. I turn my attention to the food I have."

Try taking a moment to look into the face of your kitchen goddess. Imitate her expression. What is her body doing? Mimic her position. Notice how it feels to hold your hands and arms, your legs and feet, the way she does: most goddesses have very powerful stances. Now light a candle at her feet, and enjoy the glow, the way it lights her face. Breathe deeply and quietly for a few breaths.

The final step of any kitchen ritual involves food. Allow thoughts of the food you have on hand to simply be in your mind. What hungers are stirring in you? What sounds good? Do any particular foods appeal to you now?

The seasonal sections that follow will give you lots of inspiration. You may find that the images, flavors, and sensual delights of each will keep you company throughout your rituals, suggesting many delicious ways to enjoy the rich gifts of the Earth.

KITCHEN OF THE GODDESS

I came to your warm round hut where the cooking fire spat and crackled.
You showed me the tower of brown bowls tilted crazy against the skin of wall.
"This spoon," you said, and put it, smooth from years of use, into my hand.

You scooped up something from a broad green leaf on the floor,
sprinkled it into the bubbling black pot.
Hesitant, I lowered the spoon into the stew or soup, whatever it was,
and stirred.
My muscles began to remember.
I stirred for a long time
and then I raised a spoonful to my lips—
the steamy smell drenched my mouth with moisture,
moistness flowing from mouth to mouth below,
and everything between was wide awake.
I was a baby crying for the breast.
I was open, I was starving, I had been starving for so long.
She held me in her arms as I ate. She was the ground.
She was the food. She was the spoon. She was the fire.

PART TWO

*The Earth
Mother's Seasons*

AUTUMN

The air has an exhilarating tingle, nights grow longer and, gradually, the trees reveal their inner flame. In this season of change, we can feed our Autumn hunger with the help of these magic words:

Autumn's watchwords—harvest, thanksgiving, glowing, savory, bountiful, richness, golden, comforting

Autumn scents (that evoke the splendors of Fall)—burning leaves, fresh pumpkin, the mouth-watering tartness of crisp apples or fresh cider, savory onion and squash stews bubbling on the stove, apple pies baking

SETTING THE STAGE FOR AUTUMN

The perfect autumn house is planted in a stone-edged field near the woods. You can smell smoke from a bonfire as you walk up the cobbled drive, your basket filled with apples from the tangled orchard across the lane. Indoors, you can still hear the insistent song of the stream, always on its way to somewhere, murmuring nearby. You look out through wide windows ablaze with trees. In the field, a flock of geese rests near a deep, still pond.

The autumn house glows with thankfulness and a sense of deep security. The harvest is in, the larder is filled to bursting with food, and reminders of the Earth Mother's bounty are everywhere: the autumn kitchen has bittersweet branches or swags of grapevine crowning the cabinets, earthen pitchers bursting with dried weeds in all their fragile and fascinating variety, butterscotch chrysanthemums and wild asters blooming in salt-glazed pots. Pumpkins squat, heavy-bellied, on fans of brilliant leaves. Great wooden bowls overflow with autumn squash, and baskets of acorns and nuts load the big wooden table; apples, grapes, and pears spill from cornucopias; native corn, in a magical bunch of three, casts its autumn blessing over the open hearth.

The hearth-fire burns with a gentle golden warmth, and you sit beside it for a moment to warm your hands and to gaze into the embers. What magical pictures wait for you there? What soothing, nourishing meals will you create from the harvest that surrounds you? When sunset comes, its colors splendid as the leaves' bright flame, you light amber beeswax candles to invite the sacred fire inside.

THE AUTUMN KITCHEN

The autumn kitchen is a place of celebration, a glowing shrine at the heart of our home that announces the harvest season with native corn hanging on the door and corn shocks in all their ragged beauty rustling nearby. Nothing gives us more satisfaction than the sight of a warm kitchen heaped with Autumn's gifts. Deep inside ourselves, where our most ancient memories still live, we feel that Winter will find us safe and well prepared.

Suddenly, food is the perfect decoration. Visits to our local farmer's market become intoxicating adventures, but we need strong arms to carry all the bounty of Autumn home! Once there, we're faced with the classic dilemma: should we eat it or save it to admire? Most of us end up buying more than we can use just for the sheer pleasure of looking at it all season long—fortunately, most autumn fruits and squashes keep well.

Many of us have fond childhood memories of trips to the country in the Fall. Nothing tasted better than the crisp McIntosh or Golden Delicious you munched as you drove home, car packed with apples and pumpkins and fresh cider. Making an autumn pilgrimage to beauty—opening your heart to the glory of the trees—can be a powerful experience, and roadside stands offer riches that taste especially sweet because of the extra effort you made to find them.

Mother Earth takes great joy in decorating the world in Fall. We can share some of her pleasure—and ally ourselves with her gracious abundance—when we choose autumn decorations and colors for our kitchens. In early Autumn, we surround ourselves with dusky burgundies and gold-tinged greens in honor of the orchard and wine harvests. You may enjoy stenciling or painting plump harvest pears or apples here and there, or devising borders of grapes and vines. Some of us can't resist displaying big bowls of artificial grapes (the real ones just don't last long enough) in all their fruity rubies, plums, and purples: a good fake can be a joy forever. Grapes are perfect little globes of autumn color, beautiful in and of themselves. But they also gently remind us that the hardships and pressures and bruisings of life help us to give our finest gifts: a cushioned grape gives no wine.

By midautumn, the trees amaze us with their brightness. We can echo their passionate splendor on our walls, doors, or cupboards with splashes of garnet or burnt orange, russet or gold. And here is a simple exercise that will deepen your appreciation of each leaf's beauty and complexity: choose a single perfect leaf from the many possibilities outdoors. Then, using a pencil, trace around its outline directly onto a painted cabinet or wall. Fill in your outline with the most vivid markers or paints you can find, doing your best to echo the leaf's vibrant coloration. You'll find that copying something from nature is a wonderful way to relax a stressed or harried mind. And the finished leaf (which may look surprisingly real) will be an autumn-long reminder of the trees.

There are many other ways to celebrate the trees in your kitchen. You could string some autumn-leaf lights above your sink, or hang a few preserved leaves over the table. (Try microwaving leaves between paper towels for a minute on each side to keep their color fresh.) The leaf-copying exercise above may inspire you to paint swirls of leaves on the walls. Some of us have even been known to scatter an armful of real ones on the floor to soften the harsh corners!

It can be very satisfying to make or find special kitchen decorations as the weather changes. Something as playful and inexpensive as a scarlet and orange maple-leaf potholder or a set of apple napkin-rings can add an autumn note of brightness to the room and to our meals. Autumn is the time for special family feasts; serving platters, plates, and bowls in autumn leaf or harvest fruit and vegetable shapes will become your celebratory feast companions year after year. (October just wouldn't be the same in our house, for example, without our special pumpkin tea-mugs.)

The squash harvest inspires us in the kitchen with shades of bittersweet, creamy pumpkin, and muted greens flushed with orange. Your Power Place may need an autumn cushion or throw in these delicious colors, or you could paint a harvest still-life on a cabinet, or frame a luscious autumn botanical print and display it on the wall.

In late Autumn, the pumpkins and midnight-black of the Halloween season wind a cloak of mystery around the room. By the end of October, the leaves outdoors are mostly brown and scattered. You could echo this new somberness of nature's color scheme with umber, chocolate, and sienna along with the traditional orange and black. Earthy colors remind us of the fertile power of Earth; even when she sleeps, fallen leaves become food for the soil.

When Samhain (the ancient name for Halloween) arrives on October 31, your kitchen altar may become an ancestor shrine, with mementos of dead loved ones, along with a traditional jack-o'-lantern, to honor this special day.

In Western European tradition, Autumn belongs to water, the element of emotions, feelings, relationships. Water's nature is fluid, flowing—and Autumn is certainly a time of flowing movement: flocks of geese and migrating songbirds, woolly bear caterpillars, monarch butterflies all seem caught in a bright stream flowing ceaselessly away. It can be soothing to include something blue in the autumn kitchen in honor of Autumn's element of water—a bright pottery vase, some lapis-colored native corn, or a cobalt roundel to hang in the window. Whenever your eye catches this blue magic, use it as a reminder to check in with your feelings. What emotions are flowing through you now?

This season urges us to look inward, to take stock, and to celebrate the strengths that will stay with us through the long Winter ahead—our loving relationships and our own inner wisdom. Many of us have rediscovered ancient divination tools—Tarot cards, rune stones, pendulums, and the I Ching—as valuable keys for contacting the deep wisdom we all possess. By finding space near our Power Place for a pouch of carved rune stones, a deck of jewel-colored Tarot cards, or even a special journal and pen, we honor our ability to see deeply, to make our inner landscape clearer to our conscious minds. Many autumn recipes take a little simmering or baking time. You can use this time to choose a rune or a card, or to write in your journal. You may find that poetry sings its way through you at this poignant and glorious time of year.

SONG OF THE EARLY AUTUMN GODDESS

Blessings of my first frost on you
blessings of the goose-stitched sky
blessings of the trees in sunset glory
and warm hearths at the end of the day.
Blessings of the harvest set before you
blessings of the food that comfort brings
blessings on the fire that stays within you
blessings on the fire that cannot stay.

Welcome back to my warm-kitchen embrace after weeks of Summer rambling abroad! Now my hearth-fires bring you solace. When the first frost jewels the morning grass, your heart begins to crave warm foods, soothing foods. My season is one of baking pies, the new crispness in the air as tart as Fall's sweet apples. When the wind hurries you home, what delicious pleasure it is to take my harvest and transform it—with the help of my kitchen magic—into savory and soul-satisfying meals.

Some of you come alive with my arrival, finding the squirrel's energy to gather and dance. But for many, Autumn brings sadness. Throughout my season, Nature's energies slowly turn from the busy activity of the outer world to the quiet, the mystery, of the inner one. No wonder you have mixed feelings about Autumn—my season is all about feelings.

Well, sit beside me in this glorious autumn wood and look around. My trees will teach you how to show your best and finest colors—and then how to let them go. My foods will comfort and strengthen you. And you will find that, although my magnificent splendor doesn't last forever, your inner harvests will.

EARLY AUTUMN RECIPES

APPLE-SQUASH SOUP

serves 6

Apples are the perfect autumn food: their tart, crisp flesh evokes the exhilarating weather, and their brilliant colors remind us of the leaves that give us their gift of glory for a few weeks before they fall. Paired with autumn squash, apples lend their sweetness to a classic savory soup, a glorious golden beginning to any autumn meal. Served with wholemeal bread and a salad, it can be a meal by itself.

2 tablespoons olive oil

1 to 2 cloves garlic, minced

1 medium onion, chopped

4 cups good vegetable broth (or more)

2 cups filtered apple cider or apple juice

2 cups diced acorn or butternut squash, peeled and seeded

1 large potato, peeled and diced (Yukon Gold is nice)

1 firm, tart apple, peeled, cored, and diced

Freshly grated nutmeg and ginger, to taste

Salt, to taste

$^{1}/_{2}$ cup light cream (optional)

Toppings (optional):

    Chopped walnuts

    Minced fresh parsley

    Dollop of sour or whipped cream

    Grated nutmeg

In a large soup pot, heat the olive oil and add the minced garlic and chopped onion.

Sauté onion and garlic until golden, then add the vegetable broth, apple cider or apple juice, diced squash, potato, and apple. Bring to a boil, reduce heat and simmer, covered, until squash, potato, and apple are tender, about 30 minutes.

Add nutmeg, ginger and salt to taste.

Puree in batches in blender, return to pot and gently reheat. You may add ¹/₂ cup of either light cream or more broth at this stage, thinning soup to the desired consistency. Serve warm, with any or all of the toppings on each serving, if desired.

NUTTY AUTUMN SALADS

This is the Season of Squirrels—we can't help but be inspired by their busy energy as they gather and store the nuts of Fall. Honor your own ability to harvest what you need—and make your salads more nutritious and tasty—by adding any of the following shelled nuts to your greens:

Almonds	**Cashews**
Pecans	**Pine nuts**
Walnuts	**Macadamias**
Peanuts	

The nuts may be chopped, halved, slivered, or left whole. You may also want to toast them in a frying pan or in a slow oven for a few minutes before serving.

CRISP CORN TARTS WITH
AUTUMN GREENS AND HAZELNUTS

makes 6 individual tarts

These golden tart shells make a pretty autumn picture heaped with succulent greens and topped with crunchy hazelnuts. Hazelnuts, traditional around the time of the Autumn Equinox, have age-old associations with wisdom and poetic inspiration. Shell a few for this special meal, but be sure to save some unshelled to tuck into a drawer or to string and hang on a wall.

You can find individual ¹/₂-cup tart tins in cookery catalogues, kitchen specialty shops, or even your local grocery store. There are also tins available that are shaped charmingly like autumn leaves.

And the possibilities for these golden shells are abundant: besides the filling suggested below, you could also heap them with Three Sisters Harvest Stew (see page 50), stir-fried carrots, steamed broccoli, or just about anything your heart desires. Or you could roll the dough out flat and cut shapes with miniature cookie cutters (leaf, apple, acorn, and pumpkin shapes are seasonal) and bake as a pretty topping for stews or potpies.

1 cup unbleached flour

³/₄ cup plus ¹/₄ cup fine cornmeal

¹/₂ teaspoon salt, plus salt to taste

10 tablespoons (1 stick + 2 tablespoons) chilled butter or margarine, cut into bits

2 tablespoons vegetable shortening

5 tablespoons ice water

1 to 2 tablespoons olive oil

1 or 2 garlic cloves, chopped

9 cups (more or less) greens, freshly washed, coarsely chopped (this is about a bunch, as sold in most markets; use kale, Swiss chard, spinach, turnip greens, or broccoli rabe—greens will reduce in volume as they cook)

¹/₂ cup chopped hazelnuts

To make the shells, in a large mixing bowl combine the flour, $^3/_4$ cup of the cornmeal, and the $^1/_2$ teaspoon salt (more, if you use unsalted butter).

Add the bits of butter or margarine, and the vegetable shortening.

Using two knives or a pastry blender, work butter and shortening into flour mixture until it looks like coarse cornmeal. Sprinkle with ice water.

Stir until dough holds together, gather into a ball, wrap, and refrigerate for at least an hour.

About half an hour before serving, preheat oven to 350°F.

Sprinkle your work surface with the remaining $^1/_4$ cup cornmeal and roll out dough as thinly as you can. Cut into shapes to fit six individual tart tins and press dough gently into tins.

Bake 10 to 20 minutes or until crisp. Allow to cool slightly and remove from tins.

Meanwhile, to make the filling, heat the olive oil in a medium saucepan over medium-high flame. Add the chopped garlic and stir until coated with oil.

Now add the greens and cook, stirring often, until crisp-tender and fragrant.

Salt to taste (you could use tamari, but it will discolor the greens).

Heap your shells with the cooked greens. Sprinkle with chopped hazelnuts and serve immediately.

THREE SISTERS HARVEST STEW

serves 4 to 6

This is a dish rich with textures and colors, and history. Many of the early Native American people who farmed this land lived by growing what they called the "Three Sisters"—corn, squash, and beans. Then the first white settlers came. The newcomers found this continent harsh and cruel; Winter brought starvation, sickness, and death to many. In a spirit of humane and openhearted generosity, Native Americans taught the settlers how to grow these three foods. They became three gifts of life.

Three Sisters Harvest Stew is a tribute to the Native Americans who helped the early settlers to survive. This season, with its images of Pilgrims and Indians and Thanksgiving feasts, invariably brings thoughts of Native Americans to mind. When we make this meal, we can bring our attention to those few who survived the coming of the white people to their land.

It is a good time to find out more about Native American issues. While the stew simmers, curl up in your Power Place and read a book about our government's treatment of indigenous people. You may be moved to sit at your kitchen table and write letters to your representatives in Washington: make your voice heard. It's too late to change the outcome of Wounded Knee, but James Bay and Big Mountain are at risk right now. Imagine the power of thousands and thousands of us writing letters from our kitchen tables as our stews simmer behind us. We can change things with our kitchen power. And we can take time today to give thanks for native teachings, then and now.

2 tablespoons olive oil

1 large onion, chopped

3 to 4 garlic cloves, chopped

1 large carrot, cut into 1-inch chunks

³/₄ cup butternut squash, cubed (or, for a quicker-cooking variation, use 1 cup yellow or crookneck squash, cubed)

1 can beans, drained (garbanzos, with their harvest-gold color, are my personal favorite, but you could try butter beans, or small red beans, or pintos—whatever pleases you)

1 cup dried giant white corn which has been soaked in cold water overnight and then simmered in boiling water until tender, about 2 hours. This adds a very chewy and unusual note to the stew. (Or, if you want to be really autumnal and adventurous—and if you would like to make a special link with the people who lived on this continent before us—you could use 1 cup dried Native American corn, treated the same way. Buy a bunch—usually sold as a door decoration—at the farmer's market, break the cobs in half and use a twisting motion to release the kernels. There are so many lovely colors to choose from! But please be sure that no weird shellacs or chemicals were added to your corn. Or, for a quicker version, use 1 cup fresh or frozen corn kernels.)

1 teaspoon crumbled dried sage

1 dried chipotle pepper (optional, but the smoky taste is reminiscent of the first hearth-fires of the season, perfect for Autumn)

Salt to taste

$1/4$ cup chopped fresh parsley

In a large stew pot, heat the olive oil Add the chopped onion and stir to coat with oil.

Sauté until golden, then add chopped garlic, carrot chunks, squash, beans, corn, sage, chipotle pepper, and salt to taste.

Simmer the stew until squash is tender, then add the chopped fresh parsley and stir thoroughly.

Serve piping hot.

SIMPLE BAKED PEARS

1 pear per person

Pears smell and taste like Autumn. Their sweetness evokes orchards of trees heavy with harvest fruit, smoke from bonfires weaving a spiral pattern between the branches, a golden sunset overhead and an exhilarating snap in the air. And the pear's shape is so superbly sensual. Many of us delight in celebrating the pear as we gradually grow to resemble one; but, after enjoying several very rich pear desserts—a buttery tart, a cake drenched in pear liqueur—I realized we don't exactly need to hurry that process along. And this recipe rates next to fresh fruit as one of the kitchen goddess's simplest recipes. Instead of spending a lot of time fussing over a fancy (and fattening) pear dessert, you can use that time to take a walk outdoors and enjoy the beautiful autumn foliage. The pears will be done by the time you get back.

1 pear, smooth and very firm

Preheat your oven to 350°F.

For each serving, take one smooth, very firm pear. Boscs are perfect for this, but you could use a red Bartlett—the color is wonderful—or any other firm variety.

While your oven is preheating, take a moment to appreciate your pear (some recipes require a little foreplay). Hold it in both hands and notice its nice, substantial heft. What does the skin of your pear feel like? (Boscs, for instance, have very dry, smooth skins). Enjoy stroking your pear and notice how the flesh of an autumn pear can be as crisp as the fall weather; imagine how it would feel if you took a bite of it now. Look at the beautiful gradations in its color and skin texture. Did you know that red Bartletts are dotted with tiny, differently colored circles? Now bring your pear close to your nose and inhale its harvest aroma.

When you have fully experienced your pear, stand it up, stem on top, in a baking pan and place it in the preheated oven. Set the timer for about 45 minutes. Know that when you get back from your walk, your pear will have transformed from a hard, crunchy fruit into a meltingly sweet and tender one. What a lovely gift from the Goddess. Enjoy it!

SONG OF THE MIDAUTUMN GODDESS

I am the one who sets the world on fire—
There is nothing more brilliant than my soaring leaves;
The bird who flies and flies forever am I.

I am the stream that flows without ceasing—
I am the blaze of glory that lasts a heartbeat and is gone;
The bearer of beauty and visions am I.

There is nothing self-effacing about me! How can I pretend to be less than I am—the most beautiful time of all? Some of you may say, "Yes, but Spring . . ." and to you I say, "Spring is lovely, but she blooms and blooms right up against the lushness of Summer. My beauty is all the more intense because you know Winter will be coming soon."

Have you ever tried to grab a falling leaf as it dances free from the branch? It spins and swirls and twirls away from you, always just beyond your grasp—and then, suddenly, it is lying on the ground. That is just like my season, everything dancing and rushing by. One moment, the trees are green; close your eyes and they've changed overnight. And then the leaves start falling, falling—and all at once the dance is over and the world is still. If only you had more time to pay attention! Appreciating me really should be a full-time job.

But I can be satisfied with your appreciation of my foods. I am the Great Harvest—I ask only that you enjoy me. My foods are gifts for your bodies and your souls, gifts of comfort and nurturing. You cannot hold me for long, but I will hold you forever. And the sunset beauty of my time has a sweetness like no other.

KITCHEN RITUALS FOR
THE AUTUMN EQUINOX

Sometime between September 20 and 23, a moment of perfect balance between light and dark occurs. The Autumn Equinox celebrates the day and night in equilibrium—after this day, the nights will grow gradually longer, but now the day and night are of equal length.

On this day of balance, it will help us to stay balanced in the kitchen if we take some time to weed out the things we never use. As we watch the spiral dance of the leaves, so beautiful as they let go, we can take a lesson from the trees and learn how to let go of things that we don't need anymore—all the dusty gadgets, the electric bun-warmers, plastic spoon-rests, or rubberized tablecloths that were gifts from the well-meaning long ago. Have a trade with friends, or make a donation to a charity thrift-shop or a battered women's shelter. Getting rid of outgrown stuff gives us a wonderful cathartic feeling; it becomes a way of standing firmly where we are now and saying, "This is who I am."

Today would be a perfect day to make a place on or near your kitchen altar to honor Autumn's element. Choose a special bowl and keep it filled with water throughout the autumn weeks. Notice how quickly the water evaporates: you will need to replenish it frequently. So many of us feel dried up by the frenzied demands of our lives. Refilling your water bowl becomes a way of affirming your commitment to your own inner spring, your own inner source. You may want to float a perfect leaf on top. Or scoop out the top of an apple, place a tea-light inside, light it, and float the flaming apple in the bowl.

The Autumn Equinox brings to mind the ancient Greek story of Demeter and her daughter, Persephone, who on this day of balance must go back to the underworld, land of the dead, for her annual six-month stay. Food plays a starring role in this old myth. According to the rules of the underworld, if you eat anything while you're there, you're stuck in the place forever. Hades, god of the underworld, is smitten with Persephone; he kidnaps her and takes her there, and asks her to be his queen—and he also tries to stack the deck in his favor by continually plying her with food. Now Persephone faces a big dilemma: on one hand, she misses her mother and the beauty of the upper world; on the other hand, she wants to grow up, to be something more than just her mother's daughter. What to do? Persephone solves the dilemma by eating six pomegranate seeds. For each seed, she has to spend a month in the underworld—where she can be a queen, equal to her mother in power. And for the other six months, she can be a loving daughter in the sunlit world above ground. We can share some of Persephone's experience when we do the pomegranate meditation, below.

The myth also paints a terrible picture of Demeter's grief: when her daughter first disappears, Demeter mourns her loss with rage and despair. Demeter is an earth mother and when an earth mother gets that upset, the Earth is in trouble: before long, everything is dying. Everyone from commoners to immortals tries to get Demeter to snap out of it, but nobody succeeds—until she meets Baubo, the first comedienne. Baubo manages to get a laugh out of Demeter by hiking up her skirt and showing her vulva. If you have ever considered making or buying a Sheela-na-gig for your kitchen, today would be a good day to do it. (Sheelas are shameless goddesses, with vulvas proudly displayed. They make wonderful kitchen guardians, icons of the sacred gateway of life and the strength of female sexuality, and they offer powerful healing for patriarchal attitudes toward the female body.) Sheelas remind us of the belly laugh by reminding us of Baubo, who cheered up Demeter in the throes of the very first autumn depression. You may get some weird looks from visitors (one friend saw my Sheela on the windowsill and said, "Is that a . . . ? Is that what I think it . . . ? Never mind."), but your Sheela is bound to evoke some humor and womanly power in your kitchen.

Long before the Pilgrims initiated Thanksgiving, the Autumn Equinox was the

Western European time to give thanks to the Greater Power for harvests of many kinds. Giving thanks for the blessings of the earth can be done in many and varied ways. You could make up a special blessing to say before your meal today. Persephone became a visionary—and a queen—through the choices she made. What choices have you made? What are your gifts? What have you done? Your works, like the glorious colors of the leaves, can shine brightly for awhile before Winter comes to teach us how to rest. Write a list of all the things you have in your life for which you are truly grateful, all of your personal harvests. When you are finished, fold up your list and place it on your kitchen altar with thanks.

You could also take a minute or two for this simple Autumn Equinox ritual: stand on your kitchen floor with your feet about shoulders' width apart and your weight balanced evenly. Hold an apple in one hand and a pomegranate in the other. Close your eyes and feel the weight in your hands. Is one side heavier than the other, or are they about the same? Among other things, the pomegranate is a symbol of the descent into the underworld in Autumn; the apple, of the promise of life's return in Spring. Imagine yourself as the moment of balance between light and dark, day and night, life and death. How can we learn to welcome the time of dreaming and rest as well as the time of growth and renewal? How can we honor them both?

POMEGRANATE MEDITATION

Pomegranates are magical fruits, not only because of their link with Persephone and her annual stay in the underworld, but because of even older associations with the womb, the sacred chalice of life. Grocery stores usually carry pomegranates at this time of year: you could buy two and bring them home. Place one on your kitchen altar to dry, and refrigerate the other to keep until you have a little time. Then, when you do, retrieve it from the fridge, sit comfortably at your table and regard this pome-

granate. Red and a little lumpy, its globular shape is certainly womblike. Its waxy smooth skin, when dried, will become rough and leathery. It has a jagged crown at its top, filled with tiny golden, strawlike fibers with round-tipped heads.

With a sharp knife, cut a vulva-shape gently through the surface of your pomegranate's skin—a curved diamond-shape with tips pointing up and down. Carefully peel off the skin inside this shape. The inner skin is yellowish white; it clings to the seeds like a caul around a newborn baby. When the inner skin is peeled away, the vivid seeds are exposed. Take time to appreciate the beauty of this female symbol which you have uncovered and which the pomegranate embodies. Really look at the seeds: notice their translucence, their garnet color (the word *garnet* comes from the word *granatum*, the Latin for pomegranate). If you cut one, it bleeds. It has a subtle scent. How could you describe it?

Now pry one seed gently from its socket and taste it. (In just this way did Persephone taste her first seed in Hades.) Its outer flesh is cool and sweet, but the inner seed is hard and bitter. It is certainly both sweet and bitter to be a woman in our culture today. It is sweet and bitter to be a daughter. In what other ways can you describe the lesson of the seeds for yourself? If you count out five more seeds and eat them, think of them as your tickets to the inner world, the deep, underground wisdom that the outer world of frantic busyness often makes us forget. You have become a Persephone in your choice to go deeper.

Continue to peel away the outer skin to free the seeds inside. You can eat as many as you like, saving some to make Persephone Salad (see page 61). How do you eat your pomegranate? Do you crunch up the inner seeds and outer flesh together? Or do you savor the sweetness of the pulp and spit out the seeds?

You could take a small piece of paper and use pomegranate juice to draw a symbol on it that is important to you—a spiral, a triangle, a circle. You may want to place this paper, along with a few seeds, on your kitchen altar as a reminder of the pomegranate's teachings for you.

MIDAUTUMN RECIPES

DEMETER'S SOOTHING OAT-BREAD SOUP

serves 4 to 6

Bread soups were the nourishing mainstay of many a peasant village. Simple, delicious, and filling, they are the Earth Mother's answer to chilly weather. This special recipe offers Wise Woman healing for autumn depressions, with oats to soothe the nerves and sea vegetables (reminders of Autumn's element, water) to nourish you deeply.

While you cook, remember Demeter's story. You could put a small bowl of this soup outside for her when it's done.

2 tablespoons olive oil

1 medium onion, chopped

2 or 3 garlic cloves, chopped

1 quart good-quality vegetable broth

$^{1}/_{3}$ cup crumbled dried seaweed (kelp, kombu, wakame, or dulse)

2 to 3 cups stale oat-based bread, torn into pieces (use homemade or farmer's market bread, if possible: this bread should have real body. If oat bread is unavailable, use wheat bread and add $^{1}/_{2}$ cup rolled oats to broth along with the bread.)

1 cup chopped greens (kale, collards, Swiss chard, or spinach)

1 teaspoon crumbled dried rosemary

Salt or tamari to taste

In a large soup kettle, heat the olive oil. Add the chopped onion and garlic and sauté until golden.

Add the broth and seaweed and bring to a boil. Honor the sea and the cycles of the tides as you add the seaweed to your soup.

When broth is boiling well, add the torn pieces of bread.

Turn heat down to low and simmer, stirring often, until the bread has broken down. (Just like Demeter; when *she* got depressed, the whole world died. At this point, take a look at your Sheela-na-gig and have a good belly laugh to cheer you both up.) The mixture will begin to resemble thick soup instead of broth with bits of bread in it. If soup is too thick and sludgy, thin with a little extra broth.

Add the greens and rosemary (for remembrance—think of Summer's passing as you sprinkle it in). Continue cooking until greens are just wilted.

Add salt or tamari to taste and serve hot.

PERSEPHONE SALAD

Garnet pomegranate seeds dot this pretty salad, made in Persephone's honor. All of us—no matter how close we were to our own mothers—have had to choose our own lives, our own separateness. With thoughts of mothers and daughters in our hearts, Persephone Salad becomes a thoughtful meditation on self-empowerment, wise choices, and the loving bonds of relationship.

Curly red lettuce
Pomegranate seeds
1 crisp apple

For each serving, take a few leaves of curly red lettuce. The tinge of red on the edges of the lettuce reminds us of the leaves beginning to flush and brighten outside our windows. Arrange the leaves beautifully on a salad plate and sprinkle with a handful of pomegranate seeds. (Use the leftovers from the Pomegranate Meditation, page 56. As you sprinkle, think of Persephone's decision to journey deeper, to seek her own power in the underworld. Think about your own inner journey at this time of year.)

Slice a good, crisp apple in ¼-inch slices, *crosswise*. Surprise! There is a little five-pointed star of seeds in the center of each slice. This pentacle inside the apple is a traditional symbol of health, life, and protection, the Earth Mother's promise of Spring's return. Tuck two or three slices of apple underneath the lettuce, so the edges are peeking out. (And be sure to hang a slice or two up to dry: they make beautiful ornaments for the kitchen and, later, your Yule tree.)

Drizzle with Persephone's Autumn Dressing (next page) and serve.

PERSEPHONE'S AUTUMN DRESSING

enough for 4 servings

This dressing combines fruity olive oil and a little fruit wine for a fresh zesty taste. Look for a good-quality variety. There are several Vermont vineyards, for instance, that produce nice apple/blueberry or apple/blackberry combinations; their musky-sweet taste reminds us that the wine harvest comes at this time, just as the last fruits and berries are being gathered.

> **¹/₃ cup fruity olive oil**
> **2 tablespoons fruit wine (if unavailable, use 1 tablespoon apple
>   cider mixed with 1 tablespoon apple-cider vinegar)**
> **Salt and freshly ground black pepper to taste.**

Combine the oil and wine and whisk until smooth. Whisk in salt and pepper to taste.

AUTUMN CHARD

serves 6

Chard, also known as Swiss chard, is a lovely autumn green. Like kale, it can survive a few frosts quite nicely. And the succulent leaves with their streaks of vibrant red are another vivid reminder of the leaves changing color outdoors. This chard recipe adds a creamy sauce to basic steamed greens; for those of us who feel a little blue in Autumn, this soothing, nourishing sauce can be a comfort. And its nuttiness is another reminder of the squirrels' harvest and our own gathering-in as Winter approaches.

> **8 cups Swiss chard**
> **Creamy Cashew Sauce (below)**

Wash and coarsely chop the Swiss chard. If the stems are tough, remove them and reserve for use in stir-fries, broths, soups, or stews.

Place chopped leaves in a steamer over boiling water and steam, covered, until tender, a few minutes at most.

Serve with Creamy Cashew Sauce (below).

CREAMY CASHEW SAUCE

This rich vegan version of the ubiquitous béchamel or cream sauce is also delicious on many, many other things. Try it on cauliflower, spinach, toast, baked or mashed potatoes, rice, or sautéed or other steamed vegetables. (Or, imagine an autumn version of Hot Summer Peach Play for Lovers with warm Creamy Cashew Sauce. It would be incredibly messy but lots of fun.)

> 3 tablespoons olive oil
> 4 to 5 tablespoons whole wheat flour
> 1 to 2 cups hot water
> 2 tablespoons cashew butter
> 1 to 2 tablespoons tamari
> Freshly ground black pepper to taste

In a heavy saucepan, heat the olive oil. Slowly add in the flour, stirring to make a paste, or roux. Cook for a few minutes over low heat to toast the flour and give a nuttier flavor to the sauce.

Gradually add the hot water, stirring with a whisk (amounts will vary—the end result should be a thick, creamy sauce).

Stir in the cashew butter, tamari, and pepper to taste. Mix thoroughly, pour over chard, and serve immediately.

STUFFED ACORN SQUASH

serves 6

This beautiful dish lends itself to infinite variations, all of them delicious. Try substituting 2 cups chopped kale for the cubed squash, and cornbread for the stale French bread. Or you could make this a very quick recipe by microwaving your acorn halves (10 minutes on high power or until tender) and mounding them with just about anything you have on hand: leftover Three Sisters Harvest Stew (page 50) or Lovable Lentils (page 76), or one of those great packaged wild rice or pilaf mixes with a few chopped nuts added, or some sautéed greens—if it sounds good to you and you have it on hand, it will probably work. And the acorn squash bowls, besides adding earthy flavor and creamy texture, will make any choice look delightfully autumnal and festive.

3 good-sized acorn squash

4 to 6 tablespoons butter or margarine

2 garlic cloves, minced

1 medium onion, chopped

1 medium carrot, scrubbed and diced

1 celery stalk, strings removed, diced

1 cup cubed squash (pumpkin, butternut, acorn, Hubbard, or kabocha)

1/2 cup diced mushrooms

3 to 4 cups stale French or country bread, torn into bite-sized pieces

2 eggs, lightly beaten (optional, but they give great texture to the final product)

1/3 cup chopped fresh parsley

1/4 cup chopped fresh sage (or 1 to 2 tablespoons crumbled dried leaf sage)

1/3 cup chopped nuts (optional)

2 cups (or more) good vegetable broth, salted to taste

1 cup (or more) hot apple cider or sweet white wine (optional)

Preheat oven to 350°F.

Wash whole acorn squash and cut into halves lengthwise. (This will make 6 bowls.) Remove seeds and stringy stuff and set cleaned acorn halves aside.

In a heavy skillet, heat the butter or margarine. Add the garlic, onion, carrot, celery, cubed squash, and mushrooms. Sauté this mixture over medium-high heat until vegetables are tender.

In a large bowl, mix the bread pieces, eggs, parsley, sage, and chopped nuts if desired.

Add bread mixture to sautéed vegetables and stir to mix thoroughly, then add vegetable broth (salted to taste). Continue to mix, squishing with your hands if you like, and adding broth as necessary, until stuffing is very moist and soft.

Mound stuffing into squash halves, place stuffed squash bowls on large baking sheet, cover with foil, and bake in preheated oven until squash is tender and stuffing done, 1 hour or more. Or you could place stuffed squash in a baking dish into which you have poured a cup or more of hot apple cider or sweet white wine, leave halves uncovered, and baste with pan juices every 15 minutes until done.

FIG-APPLE CRUMBLE

serves 4 to 6

The voluptous shapes of ripe figs—along with their Mediterranean associations—remind us of the bounty of earth mother Demeter, making figs perfect partners to the autumn apples in this homey, comforting dish. As it bakes, enjoy the divine perfume—an aroma bound to evoke home, hearth, nurturing, and safety.

> 1 cup dried figs, stemmed and quartered
>
> 3 large, firm apples, cored and cut into slices or chunks
>
> 1/4 cup plus 1/3 cup packed brown sugar
>
> 2 tablespoons butter or margarine, melted
>
> 1 tablespoon plus 1/2 cup unbleached white flour
>
> 1/4 plus 1/2 teaspoon cinnamon or more to taste
>
> 1/2 cup whole wheat flour
>
> 1/4 teaspoon salt or to taste
>
> 1/2 cup butter or margarine, cut into bits

Place figs in a small bowl with enough hot water to cover. Let steep until softened, about 20 minutes. Drain thoroughly.

Preheat oven to 350°F. Butter a 2-inch-deep, 8-inch-square baking pan.

In a large mixing bowl, mix apples, 1/4 cup packed brown sugar, 2 tablespoons butter or margarine, 1 tablespoon unbleached white flour, and 1/4 teaspoon of the cinnamon. Transfer apples to baking dish, and arrange figs evenly over them.

To make topping, in another mixing bowl, combine the whole wheat flour, 1/2 cup unbleached white flour, 1/3 cup packed brown sugar, 1/2 teaspoon cinnamon, or more, to taste, and the salt to taste. Using a pastry blender or two knives, cut bits of butter or margarine into this mixture until it resembles coarse meal. Sprinkle topping over apples and figs.

Bake in preheated oven until topping is golden and apples are tender, about 50 minutes. Serve warm.

SONG OF THE LATE AUTUMN GODDESS

The year's wheel turns beneath my cloak.
Wishes rise on the bitter smoke.
Winter descends with the dark.

Stir my cauldron round and round.
All that's lost is surely found.
The world sleeps, sweet is the dark.

Autumn rains and wind have taken most of the leaves from the branch, the air is damp and chill. But I can see golden lamplight from my perch high on this wind-soaked hill—your kitchen windows are blazing and bright, and something delicious is bubbling on the stove. I'm tempted to come sit by your fire and warm my old bones. Would you welcome me?

I could sing a song of bones and crones tonight, for Samhain is the crone's time and I am the Mother of all Crones. Your culture may have given me a bad rap ("hag" used to be a term of respect, can you believe it?*) but there's a whisper of the old magic in the air on Halloween that gives me hope for you, and for your daughters and sons. Your kitchens give me strength, with their pumpkins and candles and mementos of the dead. And how wise you are to cook such warm, comforting food, now that the Sun shows her face for such a little while, growing paler every day.

Perhaps food can show you how to make friends with me. I may look a little scary at first, with my bony face and my deep-black hooded cloak, but I am a loyal friend to those who understand me—I can help to set you free. When you stop being afraid of aging and death, then you can live more fully, more deeply, every moment. Honor me with special foods and rituals at least

*It meant "holy woman," and your word "hagiology" still refers to the study of saints and holy matters.

this one day every year, and when it is your turn to come to me, we will greet each other like the
dear old friends that we are.

KITCHEN RITUALS FOR SAMHAIN

The ancient Celts called Halloween by a different name. To them it was *Samhain* (pronounced "sowen"): New Year's Eve, a celebration of the dead, and a day for magic and divination all in one. Christian Western Europeans called the day that followed it All Hallows and observed it with masses and mourning for the departed. Modern-day Mexicans call it the Day of the Dead, a day for partying and tidying the graves of relatives, eating skulls made of sugar, leaving offerings for dead loved ones.

Today, the abundance of witch figures may remind us of a time long ago when the Crone or wise woman was revered instead of feared; glimmering jack-o'-lanterns are dim echoes of the candle-lit spirit-guides that welcomed back dead relations for a little visit. Halloween, like several of our cultural holidays, still has some of the magical husk surrounding it, although much of the real juice has been drained away. But with the help of the kitchen goddess (and a little autumn water-magic), we can refill Samhain from the sacred spring that never runs dry.

Samhain is both mysterious and friendly, an opportunity for us to come to an amicable understanding with death. In our culture—at once violent, death-haunted, and death-denying—we are taught to hate and fear death. Samhain helps us to make friends with it—and to honor Mystery.

We can start recreating the Halloween holiday in the kitchen. Some of us like to hide little memento mori throughout the room on Samhain. Then, whenever we open a drawer—surprise!—there's a skull grinning up at us! Skeletons may lurk among the chrysanthemums, or peek out from behind the butternuts, or dangle from a cabinet-pull, or sit with legs casually crossed waiting atop plates inside dark cupboards. The element of the unexpected adds a lot to these gentle, humorous reminders of mortality.

Our kitchen altars are the right place for old photos or keepsakes that remind us of those who have died; Samhain is the time for making ancestor shrines, in the kitchen or anywhere else. Who were your relations? Where did they come from? How did they cook, what foods did they eat?

Today is the perfect day to set the table with those old plates or glasses that were left to you by your grandmother, your aunt, or your mother. Or try using some of their utensils. If you juice the lemon for Autumn Cider Dressing with an old wooden reamer—one that was held and used by someone you loved—it will be a much more meaningful process than simply getting out the electric juicer.

You could design an entire meal around the favorite recipes of your dead loved ones (see Ancestor Feasts, page 25). Set an extra place for anyone who died in the past year, or for a special relative or friend. Tell loving stories about them at dinner.

And Samhain is the prime time for deep seeing, divination, magical workings and rituals of all kinds. Instead of making Halloween a holiday focused on sugar and scariness, we can remember the sacred roots of this night and try the magical recipe that follows.

SCRYING BREW

The ancient Celts knew that spirits were near on Samhain, that magic was as thick as sweet-smelling smoke, perfuming the air with possibilities. This Celtic New Year's Eve is the perfect night for divination. The loving ancestors who surround you like a warm cloak to keep away the winter chill will look into the future with you to see what gifts and lessons lie in store, what choices you can make to ease the way.

While many of us spend time with our rune stones and Tarot cards tonight, there is an even simpler way to dialogue with the inner self, something that doesn't require any purchased cards, stones, or other props. It's called *scrying*, and it's something our own ancestors knew how to do. Scrying is simply gazing at any dark surface until mental chatter ceases and consciousness shifts. Wisdom may come in the form of actual images that seem to take shape on the surface, or pictures or words that form in your mind. Just about anything can be used as a scrying surface—the much-touted crystal ball is one possibility, as are elaborate scrying mirrors. But even simple country people knew how to scry using pools of water, bowls of broth—or cups of tea. The following special tea will actually help you to scry. Its primary ingredient, the herb mugwort, is the divination ally of choice; so you can drink most of what's in your cup and then scry into the remainder. Happy Samhain!

The herbs are available from your local natural foods store, or from herbal companies by mail.

For each serving, boil:

1 cup water

Add boiled water to a teapot in which the following have been placed:

3 tablespoons or more dried mugwort (not only good for helping us to contact our inner wisdom, it's also very relaxing)*

¹/₄ cup dried oatstraw (good for the nerves. If all the Halloween partying and trick-or-treating have left you feeling frazzled, oatstraw will be a comfort to you.)

1 piece of cinnamon stick, 2 to 3 inches long (for its delicious flavor)

Steep for at least 15 minutes. Strain and pour into a dark-colored mug, preferably black. Sweeten with maple syrup, honey, or brown sugar, if desired.

Now, sit comfortably in your Power Place with your cup. Sniff your Scrying Brew, feeling the steam, warm as a breath, on your face. Take a sip and savor the earthy

---

*As with any herb, individual reactions may vary. If you are pregnant, nursing, or using medication, approach mugwort with caution and respect.

taste. As you sip, become aware of your breathing. Is it shallow or deep, quick or slow? As you drink, be with your breath, without attempting to change it. When the tea is nearly gone, gradually turn your attention to the surface of the liquid remaining in your cup. Gaze at it without effort, simply letting yourself be with the cup and the tea. The disc where tea meets air may look silvery if it catches a light's reflection. As you look, pay some dreamy attention to the thoughts that flash through your mind like fish. What are they? All over the world, people are scrying and dreaming tonight. What images do you see? Take as much time as you can. You may want to leave the remainder of the tea in its cup on your kitchen altar as an offering for your long-forgotten kindred who knew how to do this ancient ritual.

LATE AUTUMN RECIPES

CAILLEACH (KALE-LEEK) SOUP

serves 6 to 8

The Cailleach is a Celtic Crone figure. Samhain is her night: her strength grows with the setting sun. Picture her standing atop a seaside cliff, hooded, mysterious, her cloak swirling around her as the wind rises, frost on its breath. We can imagine the Cailleach (like her relative, Cerridwen) stirring a huge cauldron, a cauldron of inspiration and rebirth. On this Crone's night of the year, as the old year dies, make this nourishing soup to strengthen you for your own journey into Mystery. As you stir your small cauldron, remember that you are the Cailleach's sister; infuse the soup with your own goddess's strength.

2 tablespoons butter or olive oil

**3 leeks, white parts only, washed well to remove grit, sliced into
⅟₂-inch rounds (let these leek-rounds be magical reminders of
the moon in your Samhain cauldron)**

1 garlic clove, chopped

8 cups good-quality vegetable broth

2 cups coarsely chopped kale

In a large soup pot, heat the butter or olive oil. Add the leeks and chopped garlic, stirring to coat with butter or oil. When leeks and garlic are golden, add the vegetable broth and bring to a boil. Turn down the heat and simmer, covered, until leeks are tender, about 15 minutes. Then add the chopped kale.

Stir your soup (with an old wooden spoon, if you have one), and as you stir visualize your own croning process. There are many, many women on the verge of croning now. Embrace your wisdom, your strength, and your passionate convictions. The Cailleach will help to show you the way.

Allow soup to simmer until kale is tender.

Serve hot in a dark-colored bowl. Float a special autumn leaf on top, if you like. Although you can't eat the leaf, its color and shape will feed your soul.

APPLE SALAD

serves 6

Apples have a long-standing relationship with Samhain. For centuries apples were used on this night to foretell the future—and to create a lot of excitement and fun. You could try some traditional apple-play as you get ready to make this special salad: twist the stem of your salad apple while rapidly reciting the alphabet. The letter you're saying when the stem breaks off is supposed to be the initial of your true love. If you're already happily mated, then make something up for your initial (let's see, I got an "h", so I'm going to be wildly happy and harmonious. Or a "u" could mean I'm uppity and unabashed. You get the idea.)

> Autumn Cider Dressing, below
>
> 1 tart, firm red apple, cored and cut into 1/2-inch chunks
>
> 3 cups (more or less) Romaine lettuce, washed, trimmed, and torn into bite-sized pieces (you may substitute endive, if you wish, or red lettuce—whatever strikes your fancy)
>
> 1 cup arugula, washed and torn into bite-sized pieces (or you could use watercress instead)
>
> 3 tablespoons coarsely chopped walnuts (or pecans)

In a small bowl, toss the apple chunks with 2 tablespoons of Autumn Cider Dressing.

Place the lettuce and arugula in a large salad bowl and toss with the remaining dressing.

Divide the greens among 6 salad plates, top with the apples, and sprinkle with walnuts (or pecans).

AUTUMN CIDER DRESSING

1/4 **cup fruity olive oil**
1 **tablespoon apple cider**
1 **tablespoon cider vinegar**
2 **teaspoons freshly squeezed lemon juice**
1 **teaspoon Dijon-style mustard**
1 **garlic clove, crushed**
1/8 **teaspoon crumbled dried thyme**

Whisk all the ingredients in a bowl until creamy.

SWEET POTATO–APPLE BAKE

serves 6

This is a quintessential autumn dish, a colorful and tasty reminder of the Earth Mother's richness at this time of year. Many of us grew up with canned, syrupy yams (often dotted with marshmallows) at Thanksgiving; here, baking the potatoes with apples gives a surprising sweetness without all that cloying sugar.

6 sweet potatoes or yams
3 firm, tart apples
2 tablespoons olive oil
¼ teaspoon cinnamon
⅛ teaspoon ground cloves
Salt to taste (optional)

Preheat oven to 350°F.

Scrub sweet potatoes or yams and cut into chunks or slice into ½-inch rounds. Peel, core and slice the apples. Place sweet potatoes and apples in a baking dish.

In a small bowl, combine the olive oil, cinnamon, ground cloves, and mix well.

Drizzle oil and spices over potatoes and apples. Mix gently to coat potato-apple mixture evenly with oil. Cover dish and bake in preheated oven 1 to 1½ hours, or until tender. You will probably find that this dish doesn't need any salt, but feel free to add some to taste.

LOVABLE LENTILS IN PUMPKIN BOWLS

serves 6 to 8

This hearty, warming pottage is made especially lovable with the addition of marjoram, an herb long associated with love. Marjoram also acts as an antidepressant, making this the perfect meal for these nights when daylight saving time has gone away along with the evening light. Make a pot of it for the ones you love to remind yourself of the people and relationships that truly matter in your life. (This recipe makes a delicious soup, too: just add more broth.)

4 tablespoons olive oil

2 medium onions, chopped

4 large carrots, sliced into $1/2$-inch rounds. Enjoy these round orange reminders of the Samhain season; their brightness makes a delicious contrast to the darkness of the lentils.

3 garlic cloves, minced

2 cups dried lentils

4 to 6 cups good vegetable broth

2 teaspoons crumbled dried marjoram

Salt or tamari to taste

6 to 8 small pumpkins, hollowed out and cleaned (optional)

In a large soup pot, heat the olive oil. Add the onion and sauté gently until soft. Then add the carrots and garlic and cook, stirring, for 2 minutes. Add the lentils and stir to coat with oil, then add the vegetable broth (start with 4 cups and add more if necessary) and marjoram (as you add this, put your own loving feelings and thoughts into the pot along with the marjoram). Add salt or tamari to taste.

Bring to a boil, cover, and simmer until lentils are tender, about 1 hour. Check toward the end of the hour and add more broth if the mixture is too dry, or uncover the pot if mixture is too soupy.

Serve in individual small pumpkins (hollowed out and cleaned) for an especially charming Samhainy touch. If you don't have the time or energy to mess with scooping out pumpkins, you could always buy some pretty ceramic pumpkin bowls and reuse them year after year.

MOONY APPLE PIE

serves 6 to 8

Samhain and moons just go together, perhaps because Samhain's traditions are all about seeing with the lunar self, experiencing moonlit and magical realms. And creamy, custardy things are the perfect foods for Autumn, with their soothing textures and their associations with the element of water. This, then, is the autumnal version of a classic apple pie. The final product is moonlike and delicious.

> **1 Classic No-Dairy Crust (below)**
> **2 cups firm, tart apples, peeled, cored, and sliced**
> **¹/₃ cup raisins (optional)**
> **4 large eggs**
> **³/₄ cup maple syrup or honey**
> **1 cup plain lowfat or nonfat yogurt**
> **1 teaspoon pure vanilla extract**
> **¹/₂ teaspoon cinnamon**
> **¹/₄ teaspoon salt**

Preheat oven to 375°F.

Make one Classic No-Dairy Crust pie shell. (See recipe below; with four eggs in this pie recipe, you don't need all the butter of a regular crust.) In unbaked shell, spread the apples and raisins evenly.

In a blender, combine the eggs, maple syrup or honey, yogurt, vanilla extract, cinnamon, and salt, and blend until creamy.

Pour this custard over the apples and bake in preheated oven for about 1 hour, or until set. Allow to cool before serving.

CLASSIC NO-DAIRY CRUST

makes 1 crust

My dear friend Nadine is a vegan (as well as a Wild Woman). She tells me her Grammy, who isn't a vegan (but who may be a Wild Woman) has been whipping up these simple, delicious pie crusts since before Nadine was born and that they're the best vegan crusts ever. I agree. Double this recipe for a two-crust pie.

¹/₂ cup whole wheat flour
¹/₂ cup unbleached white flour
Dash salt
Scant ¹/₂ cup vegetable shortening
1 to 1¹/₂ tablespoons ice water

In a large mixing bowl, combine both flours and salt.

With two knives or a pastry blender, work in the vegetable shortening, then add the ice water, mixing quickly until dough will form a ball. Wrap and refrigerate until ready to use. When ready to use, roll out dough and place in a 9-inch pie plate. Voila! Your crust is ready to fill and bake.

THE EARTH MOTHER'S SEASONS

LAST WORD OF THE AUTUMN GODDESS

Just as you were getting used to my autumn rhythms, the season shifts, my sister Winter comes to greet you, and you have to learn a different song. Just remember, I will come back again in less than a year's time—and when I do, you will know me well.

Now I stir the cauldron slowly—
the broth is turning to stone.
Turn to face the Winter winds:
stories ride them, bony mares
swooping down on dark wings.
They long for the warmth of your waiting ears.
And there is peace in the stillness of snow.

WINTER

S lowly, Mother Earth shows us her beautiful bones. In this season of cold, snow, and long dark nights, we can learn to rest and be nourished when we remember Winter's words of power:

Winter's watchwords—earthy, hearty, homey, substantial, grounding, satisfying
Winter scents—woodsmoke, cinnamon and cloves, baked potatoes, evergreen branches, tangerines and oranges, spicy puddings slowly cooking

SETTING THE STAGE FOR WINTER

Tucked inside a stony cave or underneath the roots of an ancient tree, our perfect winter house is hugged by the earth, a cozy burrow lined with warm, smooth wood and roofed with snow. See yourself standing outside, knee-deep in snow on a moonless winter night. You're cold and hungry and tired. You have pushed yourself so hard that now you have no strength to continue. You need rest and mothering, warmth and deep nourishment.

When you lift your head, you see the warm golden lights from the windows of the winter house. You smell woodsmoke on the freezing air, like the scent of safety and protection. Something delicious is cooking over a fire, you can smell the juices sizzling, the stew bubbling. Your mouth waters. Somehow you find the strength to get there, to open the massive wooden door and fall inside. Warm arms receive you. You have come home.

The perfect winter home of our imaginings leads us deeper into Mystery. From the heart of stillness, we create a place of nurturing and healing, a womb of warmth where we can dream while the earth dreams, rest while the earth rests. Inside the winter kitchen, it's always warm and golden, cozy and serene. There are blazing wood-fires and soft cushions nearby, places to toast your toes and your spirit. Pots of richly satisfying tea are constantly steeping, and your favorite mug is close at hand.

Winter meals take time to simmer or bake, allowing you to dream by the window, luxuriating in the cozy warmth while the snow falls quietly outside. Deep quiet resides in the winter kitchen. You can hear a cat purring and the soft, hissing crackle of the fire. Your tired spirit wraps itself in peace.

THE WINTER KITCHEN

Earth is Winter's element. Earth is associated with the physical, the material—the body. When water turns to stone and the trees strip down to bone, Winter teaches us about honoring our bodies, caring for them—allowing them to take a healing time-out from our culture's demand that we produce without ceasing.

We can make our winter kitchens into places of rest, security, and cozy warmth, and we can celebrate the austere beauty of this season in many creative ways. When we welcome Winter's colors and shapes into our kitchens, we are really honoring the sacredness of our bodies and of the planet. The pleasures of making visual connection between ourselves and our Earth Mother are many.

Before midwinter comes to deck our kitchens with evergreen, you may want to make a place on your table for a few branches of brown, dry leaves; oak leaves, for example, often cling to the branch long after they have withered, and beech leaves often stick around all winter long—so even the tardy among us can collect a few. These leaves become rustling reminders of earth-colored beauty, even after they have died.

When all the leaves are gone, bare branches can take their place in a vase. Arranging a bare branch or a perfect rock can evoke the purity and peacefulness of a

Japanese Zen garden. Or you may enjoy creating magical little winter landscapes with rocks, moss, crystals (such wondrous bits of ice that never melt!), and twigs.

Early Winter is a perfect time to make or find an earth-toned rag rug to stand on when you cook or do dishes. As you stand on its firm softness, think of your own ability to be rooted in the earth. And we can echo the browns, grays, snow-white, and black of early winter in other ways, as well: earthen bowls filled with smooth gray stones or deliciously scented, cinnamon-colored pomander balls, hand-woven mats in winter colors, prints of winter landscapes, all help us to embrace this season of stillness and rest.

You may choose to echo Winter's message of sleep by creating a soft burrow or nest on your kitchen altar, especially if yours is a hibernating power animal. If your favorite animals stay active during the winter months, you may want to put out some food for the ones living outside your doors (see Kitchen Rituals for Winter Solstice, page 103, for more on decorating a Solstice tree with food gifts for wildlife). When you think about it, so many of our images of Winter involve beds and sleep: we say that snow *blankets* the earth; even sleet is said to create *sheets* of ice! We can warm up our kitchens and make them the perfect places to hibernate by including soft fabrics to curl up in. Our Power Place may need a special afghan crocheted by a loving granny, or a blanket woven in soft winter colors to pull over our shoulders like a prayer shawl as we sit and dream about winter meals.

When the Winter Solstice arrives, we bring our attention to the green that never dies. It is traditional and deeply satisfying to fill our kitchens with holly and the dusky *ever*-greens of pine and spruce. Evergreens are a feast for the senses: you may delight in heaping your kitchen with an abundance of sweet-smelling swags, garlands, and wreaths. And it can be merry to include a small branch or even a miniature tree on your kitchen altar. In the spirit of creating cozy burrows and nests for ourselves in Winter, you may consider transforming your kitchen into a real bower of greenery, tacking branches overhead and all around. When you light a candle (carefully) in a kitchen bristling with greens, the shadows it casts remind us of enchanted forests and fairy-tale magic.

Consider hanging reminders of the sun among the green; oranges cut into quarter-inch rounds and dried make lovely sunny decorations, or you could string the dried slices along with bay leaves or cinnamon sticks for a sweet-smelling festive kitchen garland. Dried chili peppers, hung in bunches or strings, are another food-based Yuletide decoration, and cranberries are easy to string and hang, too. If you don't want food hanging around, you could make or buy small golden sun-shapes which often come in beeswax and smell wonderful, to welcome the sun's return, and to celebrate the promise of our own energetic reemergence in Spring.

Greens in midwinter are usually enlivened by splashes of brilliant scarlet. Traditional holly berries, along with rose hips, apples, dried pomegranates, and staghorn sumac (as well as the aforementioned chili peppers and cranberries) all add notes of bright color to our festive kitchen. Bright orange—in the form of clementines, tangerines, or the fruit that gave the color its name—is another color choice for midwinter, one that echoes and celebrates the sun. Many of us keep a big bowl heaped with these healthful, cheery little sun-mimics for our snackers to enjoy after a day of sledding or skating.

We traditionally celebrate the midwinter season with liberality and bounty, a sort of sympathetic magic to invite more of the same in the new year. We can incorporate gold and silver—those ancient symbols of wealth—into our kitchens with spray-painted nuts, acorns, papier-mâché fruits, and branches. Or we can go back to the roots of the custom and hide a few real coins in the bottom of a vase heaped with spruce, or tuck a folded dollar bill in a wreath made of herbs and bay and juniper, to encourage prosperity and abundance in the coming year. Take some time in the kitchen to think about the ways in which we are truly rich. Money is often the least of our many blessings.

But, even more than the emphasis on undying evergreen and golden prosperity-magic, the Winter Solstice season is a festival of light. At the darkest time of the year we need reminders that the sun will return, that it will slowly strengthen, eventually bringing Spring to brighten our lives once again. A few extra candles (especially handmade or hand-decorated ones) make wonderful additions to our kitchens. Check the Hispanic section of your local grocery store to see if they carry large votives in glass: these make inexpensive and long-lasting decorations—just tie some raffia or ribbon around them and tuck in some sprigs of greenery or a few twigs.

Strings of electric lights, looped above the cabinets or wound around a wreath on the wall, can also be great fun. And besides the plain white or multi-colored bare-bulb types, there are some great shaped lights to choose from: chili pepper ones seem perfectly made for kitchens, and I've even seen tiny teapot lights that would look right at home over the table or sink. It is also possible to find lights shaped like various power animals (at night, my son's bedroom is brightened by a string of glowing fish).

But, while it's fun to decorate with lights and greens, it is also vitally important to honor our need for rest and stillness amid the frenzy of the cultural winter holiday. As one friend says, "The whole place gets lit up like a casino at Christmas but what I really crave is darkness and quiet." Try to take a few minutes every day for quiet time. Wait for a few minutes after dark to turn on your holiday lights. Start a simple, soothing teatime ritual to welcome children home from school on bitter cold days, or create a late-night Dark Time for yourself in the kitchen: after you turn off all the lights for bed, sit in your Power Place in the dark and breathe quietly for a few minutes. You will be surprised by the a difference those few minutes will make.

In late Winter we begin to think about emerging from our winter hibernation. You may want to include some opalescent colors in your late winter kitchen to remind you of the ice that will soon be thawing, the snow that will melt into Spring. One friend hangs crystal points around her kitchen in January like little magical icicles.

The kitchen is the perfect place for forcing a few flower bulbs placed in vases, bowls of water, or shallow bowls of smooth stones. If you start them in early January, they may bloom in time for Imbolc, inspiring symbols of life's dauntless power to return again and again.

STORY OF THE EARLY WINTER GODDESS

Not so long ago, my children knew that with winter came story-telling time: crops safely gathered in, no planting to be done, nothing but long nights made for stories and sleep. Your bodies still remember. Here is my story for you.

Once there was a man who never stopped working, from early in the morning until he fell into bed at midnight exhausted. He ate his hurried meals without noticing what he ate, for his attention was continually on the problems and challenges of his work. He barely noticed the seasons changing, certainly never noticed the moon swelling and diminishing night after night, for only work was important to him and he had no reason to look anywhere else.

One night in early Winter, when the few leaves left on the trees were brown and dry and the Air had put on her thorny cloak of cold, the man was walking home in the dark when he stumbled over something in his path. He fell heavily, for he had been thinking hard. His hand closed around the thing that had caught his foot. It was a rock, about the size of his fist. Cursing, he hurled it away from him and continued home, rubbing his bruises.

The next night, as he walked home tired and preoccupied, once again something tripped him and made him stumble. Reaching down, he found the same rock, or he thought it was the same—about the size of his fist, cold and hard as iron. "How could this thing be here again? Get out of my way!" and he threw the rock with all his strength as far from his path as he could. That night, in bed, he remembered it and cursed it as he fell into his habitual restless sleep.

The following night, as he walked home even later than usual, his mind end-lessly worrying over the latest crisis in his work, he came to the place where he had tripped twice before. There, his feet stopped still. Without meaning to, he found him-self remembering the rock. He looked down at the earth and—amazing!—there was the rock again. With a snarl, he bent over and grabbed it, intending to hurl it away again, when something—he didn't know what—stopped him. Puzzled, he shrugged, put the rock in his pocket, and soon forgot about it as he continued home.

The next day, the man went to work with the rock in his pocket. His coat felt heavier when he put it on. He found that the rock made him walk differently. When he thought about it at all, he told himself, "I'll throw it away," but something kept him from doing it. And, even more strange, when the sun set and darkness fell, the man, who was hunched over his desk as usual, found himself thinking, "I'm a lit-tle hungry. I wouldn't mind some soup. Maybe I'll go out for once instead of get-ting dinner from the vending machine. Maybe I'll go out and get a good meal." And he did.

After he had eaten, the man thought, "I almost feel sleepy, that soup was so fill-ing and good. I don't know why, but I feel like going home early tonight and rest-ing a little. Maybe I'm coming down with a cold." And he walked home and fell asleep in his chair, without even taking off his coat. When he woke, he felt more rested and happy than he had felt for a long, long time. He reached into his pocket and found the rock. He took it out and really looked at it for the first time. Then he tucked it back in his pocket and thought no more about throwing it away. Whenever he remembered it, he would reach in and touch it, and every time he did the rock was always warm to his touch.

Remember your bodies, my children. Take care of them. Feed them well. And if the demands of your lives don't allow you time to rest, at least imagine what it would be like if you could.

EARLY WINTER RECIPES

There is an old wisdom to overeating in early Winter. Just as hibernating creatures get pleasantly plump before they start their long winter sleep to ensure their survival, so our ancestors—worried about the possibility of food shortages and lean times—liked to put on as much weight as they could while food was still plentiful. While the harvest is still fresh in our minds and in our pantries, we can create special nourishing feasts, strengthening our bodies to face the cold weather ahead.

Early Winter is pumpkin season. Not only are pumpkins rich in nutrients, they have become a symbol (along with the turkey) of the cultural Thanksgiving which just wouldn't be the same without pumpkin pie, the quintessential American food. (Did you know that the early Celts carved jack-o'-lanterns from turnips, not pumpkins? Pumpkins were unknown to Europeans until colonists came to the New World.) But pumpkin has so many other delicious uses besides the traditional pie. In this section, you will find a luscious pumpkin-based soup, as well as a pumpkin pudding (which can also become a perfect pumpkin pie), but here are some other ideas to get you thinking about the beauty and flavor of pumpkins. First, the easy instructions for:

HOW TO COOK A PUMPKIN

A 6-pound pumpkin will give you about 8 cups of puree. This is a lot of pumpkin, but you can use it in some of the many ways suggested here, or you could freeze it, or share it with your friends. (Or use a smaller pumpkin: a 1¹/₂-pounder will only yield 2 cups of puree.)

Canned pumpkin may certainly be substituted for this home-baked puree if you're short on time—but this tastes so much better. And it is surprising how much more meaningful and nourishing our food is when we involve ourselves with it in this way. Baking a pumpkin becomes a reminder of the level of interaction that existed between our ancestors and their food—and if you grew your own pumpkin, so much the better!

1 6-pound pumpkin, or smaller

Preheat oven to 375°F.

Cut your pumpkin in half and place the halves facedown on a baking sheet. (If your pumpkin is very large, quarter it.) Bake the pumpkin sections in your preheated oven for about 45 minutes, or until fork-tender.

When cool enough to handle, peel off pumpkin skin, remove the seeds (for a delicious treat, bake them for a few minutes at 325°F), and scrape away the stringy stuff. Then puree the pulp in batches and use or freeze.

THINGS TO DO WITH COOKED PUMPKIN

When we include pumpkin in our early winter foods, we add creamy texture, earthy taste, and good nutrition (and your children won't even know it's in there). Try some of the variations on a pumpkin theme given below.

- You could add a half cup or more cooked or canned pumpkin to any of the following:
    Soups, stews, broths
    Pasta sauces
    White sauce (it will turn a lovely color)
    Cooking water for rice, millet, quinoa, or spelt

- Combine cooked pumpkin with the following and serve on bread, toast, or muffins, or use as an icing for cakes, cupcakes, or fruitbreads:
    Cream cheese (use more to stiffen if making icing, less for a sandwich or muffin topping)
    Maple syrup, honey, brown sugar, or applesauce
    Pumpkin pie spices—cinnamon, allspice, cloves, nutmeg

- Or try making open-faced sandwiches with cooked pumpkin and:
    Mashed cooked beans
    Grated cheese
    Chopped figs, raisins, dried cranberries, or cherries
    Chopped nuts, or toasted or raw pumpkin seeds or sunflower seeds

SMOKY PUMPKIN SOUP

serves 6

This unique and flavorful soup combines the perfection of pumpkin with the smokiness of winter hearth-fires. This recipe grew out of a soup shared with friends during a cozy fireside lunch at a nearby colonial inn. Outside, the November day was blustery and cold, but indoors the company was good and the pumpkin soup was warm and delicious. My friends tell me this version, with its unusual smoky taste, is even better than the original!

3 tablespoons butter, margarine, or olive oil

1 medium onion, chopped

2 to 3 garlic cloves, minced

1 small to medium carrot, sliced in $1/2$-inch rounds

$1/2$ cup well-scrubbed sweet potato, cut into chunks

6 cups vegetable broth

1 cup pumpkin puree (or 1 cup chopped raw pumpkin)

1 slice oat bread, torn into pieces (this adds body and oaty nourishment; if oat bread is unavailable, substitute whole wheat and add 1 tablespoon rolled oats)

1 teaspoon dried thyme

1 teaspoon crumbled dried sage

$1/2$ cup (or more) light cream or half-and-half (vegans may substitute soy milk or 2 tablespoons cashew or almond butter for a creamy texture)

$1/2$ cup smoked gouda cheese, grated (this is what gives the soup its delightful smoky flavor; vegans may use a few drops of natural smoke flavoring instead)

$1/4$ cup chopped fresh parsley

Suggested toppings (optional):

Dollop of sour cream, whipped cream, or crème fraîche

Small mound of grated smoked gouda

Grating of fresh nutmeg or a pinch of dried sage or thyme
Sprinkling of cayenne, for those who love heat
Spoonful of pumpkin seeds, raw or toasted

In a large soup pot, heat butter, margarine, or olive oil over medium flame. When butter is melted, add the onion, garlic, carrot, and sweet potato. Sauté vegetables, stirring to coat with butter, for a few minutes until onion is translucent. Add the vegetable broth, pumpkin puree, oat bread, thyme, and sage. Stir to mix thoroughly, bring to a boil, then reduce heat, cover, and simmer until sweet potato is tender, about 30 minutes.

Add the light cream or half-and-half, cheese, and parsley. Stir to mix and continue to simmer (do not boil) until cheese is melted.

Puree in batches in your blender or food processor, adding more cream to thin if needed.

Serve warm in individual bowls with a combination of any of the suggested toppings.

WINTER GREENS AND WALNUTS SALAD

serves 4

Winter greens have more body and bite than their more tender spring or summer relatives. Paired with toasted walnuts and mild red onion, this winter salad is a piquant contrast to the sweetness of roasted vegetables or pumpkin soup.

Assorted greens, rinsed clean (arugula, mustard greens, or watercress; chicory or curly endive; and romaine)

2 tablespoons chopped red onion, per serving
1 cup toasted walnuts
Olive oil
Good-quality vinegar or red wine
Salt and freshly ground black pepper to taste

Toast walnuts in oven at 300°F for 10 minutes.

For each serving, take several leaves of each of the the greens, and tear into bite-sized pieces. Mound greens on salad plates and sprinkle each serving with chopped red onion, and toasted walnuts.

Drizzle each salad with olive oil and a splash of good-quality vinegar or red wine and add salt and pepper to taste.

HEARTHA'S ROASTED WINTER VEGETABLES

serves 4 to 6

Heartha loves to keep us warm and nourished when the weather turns raw. This goddess of the hearth knows how to make a kitchen smell divine, and how to turn the simplest ingredients into luscious winter fare. This dish evokes a red-cheeked, plump, and homely goddess—a kindly, no-nonsense type—her sleeves rolled up as she cooks, her skirt the color of fallen leaves. Heartha wants to make things easy for us: her Roasted Winter Vegetables are so simple to prepare—chop a few things, toss with oil, and then go take a warm bath or a nap while the roots and legumes cook. The vegetables end up sizzling deliciously, with crusty brown outsides and tender insides—simple, substantial, tasty.

6 cups assorted vegetables, scrubbed and cut into 1-inch chunks—
choose from:

Yellow onion

Potato (Yukon Gold is pretty)

Sweet potato

Winter squash (butternut, acorn, kabocha, Hubbard)

Carrot

Parsnip

Turnip or rutabega

3 tablespoons olive oil

1 tablespoon dried rosemary

2 garlic cloves, pressed

Coarse salt to taste

Freshly ground black pepper

Preheat oven to 400°F.

Scrub and cut into uniform 1-inch chunks any or all of the vegetables listed to make up about 6 cups.

In a small bowl, combine the olive oil, 1 tablespoon dried rosemary, and garlic (or omit the rosemary and garlic and use 2 teaspoons ground cinnamon instead), and mix well.

Spread vegetables out on a large baking sheet and drizzle with herbed oil, turning to coat vegetables evenly. Sprinkle with salt and black pepper to taste.

Bake in preheated oven for about 1 hour. At this point, remove any vegetables that are done and continue roasting the rest until tender, lightly browned, and sizzly—another 30 minutes at most. Serve hot.

KALE, CORN, AND ONION SKILLET CAKES

4 to 6 servings

Corn kept many Native American people alive throughout the long winter months: dried corn that had been soaked and then cooked was a staple food. Today freezers make it possible for us to enjoy corn in all its tenderness, any time of the year; paired with winter kale, it gives a wonderful, toothy richness to these hearty cakes.

A cross between a pancake and a fritter, these cakes are quite substantial and filling.

> 1 cup all-purpose flour
> 1 cup fine yellow cornmeal
> 1 teaspoon salt, or to taste
> 2 cups frozen corn, thawed
> 2 cups finely chopped, firmly packed fresh kale
> 2 large eggs
> 2 tablespoons melted butter or olive oil
> 2 cups lowfat or nonfat milk
> 2 tablespoons olive oil or butter
> 1 cup diced onion

In a large bowl, mix the flour, cornmeal, salt, corn, and kale.

In a medium bowl, beat lightly the eggs, 2 tablespoons melted butter or olive oil, and milk to combine. Pour wet ingredients into dry and mix briefly.

In a large skillet, heat the remaining 2 tablespoons butter or olive oil. Add the onion and sauté until golden.

Add sautéed onion to batter, mix again, then drop about ¼ cup batter per cake into hot skillet, adding more oil as needed to keep cakes from sticking. Cook until cakes begin to bubble, about 3 minutes, then flip and cook until the other side is golden, 1 or 2 minutes longer. Serve warm.

PUMPKIN PUDDING (OR PIE)

serves 6

This is an undeniably rich dessert, but it is also undeniably delicious; after all, a few extra treats (and pounds) are always in order in Winter. And Pumpkin Pudding translates beautifully into a perfect pumpkin pie: although you don't really need *the extra calories of a crust, you could throw caution to the wintry winds and indulge yourself and those you love.*

This is just about the simplest way to make a pumpkin pudding (or pie), ever. The blender becomes a true genie, magically whipping up this wintry dessert with the push of a button or two. (To minimize the toxins found in dairy fat, use organic dairy products if at all possible.)

$1^3/_4$ **cups pumpkin puree**
$^1/_2$ **cup brown sugar**
$^1/_4$ **cup white sugar**
$^1/_8$ **cup maple syrup**
$^1/_2$ **cup sour cream**
$^1/_2$ **cup heavy cream or half-and-half**
2 eggs
1 teaspoon cinnamon
$^1/_2$ **teaspoon ground ginger**
$^1/_4$ **teaspoon salt**
$^1/_8$ **teaspoon ground cloves**
Whipped cream (optional)

Preheat oven to 425°F.

Just dump all the ingredients (except whipped cream) in a blender and pulse until thoroughly combined.

Pour mixture into buttered individual ramekins or ovenproof soup bowls—or the unbaked pie shell of your choice. (Decorate with little leaves cut from pastry, if you like.)

Bake for 15 minutes at 425°F, then reduce heat to 350°F and bake for 45 more minutes, or until set. Enjoy the spicy smells that, like incense, turn your oven into a sacred shrine.

Allow to cool for about 1 hour before serving. This dish is certainly rich enough—and scrumptious enough—all by itself, but feel free to top each portion with whipped cream, if you crave it.

STORY OF THE MIDWINTER GODDESS

I know how tired many of you feel, your poor bodies practically pulled apart with the extra strain and stress of holiday time, all those conflicting demands, when what you really need is more sleep. Well, curl up in a comfy chair and rest for a minute. I have a story of healing for you.

Late one cold December night, a woman left her house, which was crowded with people, and stepped outside for a moment of peace. Behind her she could hear the noise of many voices, the electric chatter of the television, and the stereo's insistent whine. She shut the door behind her. She drew in a deep breath.

Outside it was very, very still. No wind. No moon. No light anywhere. She walked a few paces away from the throbbing house and sat on the cold, bare earth, her head pillowed on her arms, her arms pillowed on her knees. Without thinking, she reached one hand down and touched the earth. It was dark and hard and unyielding. Her fingers closed around a lump of earth that was even harder than the rest. She sat for a moment with her fingers wrapped around this piece of earth, drinking in the quiet and the darkness. When she sighed and pushed herself off the ground to go back indoors, she took the bit of earth with her.

Later, after everyone had fallen asleep, the woman had a chance to examine the piece of earth she had brought inside. It was a lump of coal, smooth and shiny as jet. Smiling, she remembered childhood threats of Santa with his lumps of coal for naughty children. This bit of coal was as beautiful as a jewel.

The woman turned it this way and that, delighting in its earthy depth and darkness. She remembered the peace she had felt as she sat outside in the place where the coal had been at home. Gradually, as she remembered and dreamed, she became aware of a pulsing beneath her fingers, as if a living heart beat inside the coal, or a living flame danced inside it. "Keep this stone as a talisman," said a voice in her mind. "The secret of its earthy darkness and living flame are dearer than diamonds." She placed the coal on her kitchen countertop, where she passed it and noticed it often.

The next day, as she hunted in her refrigerator for something to cook, she came across a few root vegetables: a beet, a carrot, a turnip. She picked them up and, as she held them, she began to feel the same mysterious darkness alive in these foods that had once grown—like the coal—in the earth, the same living flame at their heart. She cooked and ate them with gratitude, aware that their good, grounded nourishment would help her face the stresses of her life. Soon she began to celebrate the earthy strength and dancing flame that she carried in her own body, in her own heart.

Solstice is the living flame at the heart of dark, earthy Winter. My foods will help you to get through this difficult, beautiful time with inner peace and outward joy. You are all my precious Solstice flames. I love to feed you. And I love to see you shine.

MIDWINTER MEDITATION: EATING THE EARTH

This meditation gently brings us into awareness of the earth and of our bodies. It can be an especially powerful exercise when done in near darkness, perhaps by the light of a single candle. Choose a time when you have an hour or so to spare: potatoes have a lot to teach us about slowing down and grounding.

First, choose a medium-sized baking potato, and start preheating your oven to 425°F. Take your potato with you to your Power Place and get comfortable. Now, touch your potato. Is it gritty? There may be bits of earth, like tiny crystals, still clinging to it. Imagine how the potato grows, underground in the dark, quietly swelling. Feel all the intriguing lumps and bumps, the little crevices and hills, of your potato. Potatoes are as variable in shape as the land. Feel the comforting, substantial weight of the potato in your hand. One potato can nourish and fill you for hours. Once, potatoes kept starvation at bay for millions of people. And when blight hit the crop, the people died.

Breathe with attention for a moment, simply noticing the pattern of your breathing, the taking in, the letting go, over and over, effortlessly. Now, as you continue to breathe gently and naturally, bring your awareness to the center of your chest. Allow that center to feel warm and open. Now begin to think of the people alive today, this moment, who are hungry: some are far away in places you can only imagine. Others live nearby. Think of what a great blessing it is to have enough to eat. As you hold your potato, think of solid, practical ways that you can help. Do you have any extra canned goods? You could take them to a homeless shelter later. Or you could volunteer some time cooking a holiday meal for the needy in your area. (Friends report that their most meaningful and joyful holidays were spent giving themselves in service in this way.) When we have enough, we can share what we have, whether it's a gift of

time or food or money. Take a moment to breathe your gratitude for having enough, your gratitude for this simple, earthy potato that, in its unassuming but powerful way, sums up the food that is there for you whenever you are hungry, whenever you need it.

Now, really look at your potato. It has individuality, character. Its body will become a part of yours. This is the way of life on Earth, bodies continually giving themselves to other bodies, eater and eaten in a circle dance. When you bring your potato to your nose, can you smell its subtle, earthy scent?

Once your oven is preheated, wash your potato, enjoying the way water brings out the smoothness of its skin. Pat it dry. Place it in your oven, and set the timer for 45 minutes.

In that 45 minutes, sit quietly in the dark and take note of how your body feels. Do you hold any tension or pain anywhere? Bring your attention to those places and simply be with the feeling there. Place your hands on the place, if you can, and breathe quietly, not willing anything to happen, just allowing the energy that flows through all creation to flow through you. If your body is feeling relaxed and comfortable, simply take note of that, and enjoy the pleasure of being without pain, without stress. Allow yourself to feel cradled by the warmth and the darkness. Close your eyes and dream, if you like.

As time flows through you, notice how the potato is beginning to fill the room with fragrance. The flesh of a raw potato is hard and crisp and pearly as an apple. Your potato is baking into softness, into mellow creaminess. When the timer rings, put on an oven mitt, remove your potato, and cradle it for awhile.

Is your potato steaming? How does it smell now? When it has cooled just enough to not burn you, place your potato on your body anywhere that you may have been feeling tension or discomfort. Enjoy the heat and steam soothing and warming your skin and muscles. Imagine the potato's sweet, earthy goodness penetrating all the way to your bones.

When you are ready, open your potato. What a burst of steam and whiteness erupts from its earthy darkness! Now sprinkle your potato with salt, and eat it. Savor each bite, knowing as you chew each mouthful that you are eating all the little hills and valleys that you felt before. The potato is a gift from the Earth Mother; know that its goodness was formed in the earth, of the Earth. Know that your body shares the potato's earthiness—we are all made of Earth's elements. And know that the Winter Solstice erupts with a burst of light and warmth out of the darkest time of the year, to bless our bodies and our souls with hope, renewal, and nourishment.

KITCHEN RITUALS FOR WINTER SOLSTICE

Sometime between December 20 and 23, the longest night of all arrives to wrap the world in darkness. The Winter Solstice celebrates the rebirth of the sun: after this darkest night, the days will slowly lengthen. The cultural winter holidays that share this Solstice time also focus on the return of light and life, the birth of something precious and holy. We discover the roots that connect all of Earth's children when we embrace the solstice holy day; it celebrates an event that is true for us all, no matter what other beliefs may divide us.

The Winter Solstice is all about honoring the dark and rejoicing in the light. Try this simple ritual on Yule Eve (the night before the Winter Solstice): sit in your Power Place at twilight. Watch the world gradually grow darker. Allow the dark to simply be in your home, in your kitchen. Notice the small sounds that fill the quiet. Be quietly with the dark. Think of the fertile, nurturing darkness of the womb. What are you gestating now? What dreams do you have for the future? What do you hope to bring forth? Think of the Earth Mother, in labor during this dark season to birth the Sunchild.

Now, light a single candle—perhaps the one on your kitchen altar. What a great difference a single candle's light can make! Enjoy the warm glow. Really notice the different colors that lie at the heart of the flame. Make a wish for peace. Hum an old carol. Here is an Earth-based version of a classic that we sang during a recent Winter Solstice celebration:

> Silent night, holy night,
> All is calm, all is bright
> Round yon luminous Mother and Child,
> Holy Infant so tender and wild.
> Greet the Solstice in peace,
> Greet the Solstice in peace.

Continue lighting any other candles you have placed around your kitchen. Then turn on every light in the room. Make noise if you like. The light *does* return, year after year. We can honor the darkness, and we can be grateful for the light.

Now, as you walk the circle of your kitchen extinguishing all but the most necessary lamps or candles, ask yourself, What are the lights in my darkness? What are the things that shine brightly for me? We are all alive on this planet at this moment. What a strange and wonderful combination of personalities and talents and gifts we represent. How can we shine for the world?

On the day of the Solstice, we can make a conscious connection with our planet by taking a walk outside to discover a kitchen stone: any rock that is pleasing to you will do. Bring your stone inside, wash it off, and place it on or near your altar to remind you to stay in touch with the Earth, to stay grounded and aware of your body. You may replace this rock every year on the Solstice, returning last year's kitchen stone to the earth.

Another kindly Solstice tradition is decorating an outdoor tree with food gifts from your winter kitchen: such Solstice trees are a delight to watch, as squirrels and birds come to share the festival that humans have celebrated for centuries. Pinecones spread with peanut butter and rolled in seeds and cranberries, orange halves filled with nuts, dried fruit, ears of dried corn—all make pretty, delicious decorations for the animal people around you.

Today is a good day to perform a simple blessing over your food. Your body's own wondrous energy will do the blessing for you if you simply hold your hands over what you are about to eat. Hands helped to plant and nurture this food. Hands helped to harvest and package it. Hands cooked it. And the goodness of the food will strengthen us, hands and all.

Even in this time of stillness and rest, the Mother of the Wild offers us nourishment for body and soul. Try the following special winter tea for a lively and delicious taste of the untamable green.

WHITE PINE TEA

During the winter holiday season most of us invite the living green of pine, spruce, and fir indoors—in the form of wreaths and decorated trees, garlands and centerpieces—where their uplifting scents and vivid colors are infinitely cheering during these short, cold days. But we can also drink the energy of the deathless evergreen, sending its message of hope and renewal to our bodies in a very basic and earthy way.

The tangy sharpness of this tea is delightful to children and adults alike. The whole family can get involved in its gathering and preparation; make a real celebration out of it!

If you're not sure what a white pine looks like, consult a field guide to trees. (White pines have long, smooth needles.) Then bundle up, and go to the nearest white pine (city folk may need to look in parks for theirs). Try to find one that is well away from the road to avoid heavy-metal contamination from cars.

Spend a moment appreciating the beauty of the tree's glossy needles and fresh, pungent scent. Evergreens stand out like beacons of life from their seemingly dead and bare companions. Thank the tree for its gift of needles; you could leave the tree a Solstice gift of a crystal or a special stone.

For each serving of your White Pine Tea, pick:

**1 handful fresh needles (handfuls, like sizes of hands, vary—
that's fine, everybody can pick their own)**

Take your needles indoors and boil:

1 cup water per serving

Put the needles in a teapot and cover with boiling water. Steep, covered, for at least 15 minutes, then strain and serve, with sweetener, if desired.

As you sip, think of this beautiful quote from Buddhist monk Thich Nhat Hanh: "Drink your tea slowly, as if this activity is the axis on which the whole Earth revolves. Live this moment. Only this actual moment is life."

Know that this tangy, delightful tea is filled with vibrant green energy. That energy (as well as some helpful nutrients—especially vitamin C) is the tree's gift to you. May we all feel as healthy and strong as the white pine!

WASSAIL

Old-time Western Europeans were fond of greeting the Yuletide with strong drink. When revelers or carolers or merrymakers descended upon you, it was expected that you would offer a steaming cup of something to take away the chill. Wassail comes from the Anglo-Saxon *wes hal*, or "be whole," a wish for your visitors' good health and wholeness. What a much-needed and wonderful blessing for our times! We can wish each other the same in a mug of wassail today.

This recipe is rooted in ancient and traditional Yule drinks, but it changes every time I make it. Feel free to improvise, so that your wassail will be as individual and unique as you are. Any way you pour it, wassail is a proven ally in helping friends and family to make merry, and it works better than any potpourri for filling the house with delicious aroma. You could make a smaller vat of non-alcoholic wassail for children and set it to simmer on the stove alongside the grownup version. Just be sure—once you've had a mugful or two—that you don't get the batches mixed up!

This recipe serves a large gathering of moderate drinkers, or a small one of serious revelers. Measurements are approximate: the best rule is to taste and add, taste and add, until it tastes delicious.

In a large soup pot, gently heat the following ingredients:

1 gallon (or more) apple cider

1 large cinnamon stick, broken into pieces

13 allspice berrries (one for each full moon of the year)

1 apple, sliced crosswise to reveal a pentacle within each slice

1 small whole orange, organic if possible, studded with 8 whole cloves (one for each festival of the year)

Then add:

Irish whiskey (my personal favorite, but you may use other whiskeys or even burgundy or claret if you wish)

Maple syrup or brown sugar to taste

Start by adding a cup or so of alcohol to your wassail and taste to determine the potency you're after, adding more and tasting until you get it right or you're beyond worrying about it.

Do not allow wassail to boil unless you want to lose the alcohol. Serve steaming hot in mugs. You could follow an ancient custom and have your friends bring their own special wassail cups from home with them (just about anything will work as a wassail cup). As you fill their cups, add a few wishes for the coming year. Make splendid and outrageous toasts. Enjoy!

ROOT SOUP

serves 4 to 6

This tasty, earthy soup honors the darkest night of the year with its own rich color that rivals the holly berry for scarlet brightness. Based on traditional borscht recipes dear to the hearts of those who live in wintry lands, Root Soup will warm your heart and your soul. Beets remind us of the Earth Mother's blood; their deep purplish red flesh and magenta juices are so rich in vitamins and minerals that eating beets becomes a nourishing infusion, one that is sorely needed around the winter holidays.

2 tablespoons olive oil or butter
1 medium onion, diced
2 garlic cloves, minced
6 cups vegetable broth
3 cups diced fresh beets
1 medium potato, diced
$1/2$ cup diced carrot
$1/2$ cup peeled, diced parsnips
$1/2$ teaspoon dried thyme
$1/2$ teaspoon freshly grated nutmeg
$1/2$ teaspoon salt or to taste
Freshly ground black pepper to taste

In a large soup pot, heat olive oil or butter. Add the onion and garlic and sauté until softened, about 5 to 7 minutes. Then add the vegetable broth, beets, potato, carrot, parsnips, thyme, nutmeg, and salt and pepper to taste.

Bring to a boil, then reduce heat and simmer for about 45 minutes to 1 hour, until beets and parsnips are tender. Serve hot. (Some may prefer to puree their Root Soup, but I find that leaving the roots in chunks feels more earthy.)

POMANDER SALAD

4 servings

Once upon a time, oranges were nearly worth their weight in gold and were especially prized around Yuletide. (Before the Crusades, most English and other Western European people had never even seen, let alone eaten, an orange.) Rediscover the preciousness of the orange, shining like a little sun, that gives us its cheery fragrance and healthful vitamin C, Solstice gifts from the Mother-of-All.

This salad not only celebrates the orange, it reminds us of pomanders—oranges studded with cloves and rolled in spices, once prized as a kind of health protectant, deodorant, and perfume all in one beautiful package. The delicious aroma of pomanders has always made my mouth water. Now you can have your pomander and eat it, too.

> **Assorted greens (escarole, red lettuce, chicory, and/or romaine)**
> **2 seedless oranges, sliced in rounds, white pith removed**
> **1/2 red onion, minced**
> **Pomander Dressing (below)**

On each salad plate, place several leaves of greens as desired. Divide orange slices evenly among salad plates, overlapping and arranging them decoratively on lettuce leaves. In the center of each serving, place 1 tablespoon of minced red onion.

Drizzle each serving with Pomander Dressing (below). Serve immediately.

POMANDER DRESSING

¼ cup plus 2 tablespoons olive oil

1 tablespoon red wine vinegar

1 tablespoon freshly squeezed orange juice

¼ teaspoon ground cloves

¼ teaspoon salt

¼ teaspoon Dijon-style mustard

Whisk all ingredients in a bowl (or shake in a lidded jar) until creamy.

FESTIVE GREEN BEANS WITH CRANBERRIES

serves 6

Echo the colors of the season with this simple, pretty dish. If you don't have any dried cranberries on hand, you could substitute julienned red bell peppers.

3 cups green beans, washed with ends trimmed

½ cup dried cranberries

Melted butter or olive oil, as desired

Salt to taste

Place beans and cranberries in a steamer basket over boiling water and lightly steam until beans are bright green and crisp-tender and berries are plumped. Serve on a platter, drizzled with melted butter or olive oil and sprinkled with salt to taste.

SAVORY YULETIDE PIE

serves 4 to 6

Feel the power of the universe that makes the days grow longer once again, that brings light and warmth to the frozen earth. That same power flows through you. You can become the goddess Yula in the kitchen today, crowned with ivy and wielding a wooden spoon instead of a holly-tipped scepter. Use your hunger and your creativity to make a unique and sumptuous festival meal, a meal that will feed both body and soul.

The roundness of this savory pie echoes the shape of the sun that we honor at the Solstice season with lights and celebrations of many kinds. The ingredients will be up to you; every time you make this recipe, depending on what you have on hand and what appeals to you, it will taste different, but delicious. (And you don't have to spend the entire day chopping vegetables for this dish, either. It is entirely possible to make Yuletide Pie with canned and frozen ingredients and a store-bought crust, if you're just too exhausted to stand over a chopping board.)

2 to 3 tablespoons olive oil

2 to 3 cups (when cooked) diced vegetables—choose from:

Onion	Sweet potato
Garlic	Winter squash
Carrot	Turnip or rutabaga
Bell pepper	Parsnip
Celery	Broccoli
Potato	Brussels sprouts
Mushroom	

1 to 2 cups (when cooked) additional vegetables (greens will reduce in volume)—choose from:

Frozen peas

Frozen corn

Canned tomatoes (if you canned any over the summer, this is the perfect time to use them: they become warm reminders of the sun's power)

Canned or cooked beans

Chopped kale, cabbage, mustard greens, turnip greens, broccoli rabe, or chard

Suggested seasonings:

Chopped fresh parsley

Pinches of dried herbs: your choice of thyme, rosemary, sage, basil, savory, or marjoram, or a combination

Salt and freshly ground black pepper to taste

1 tablespoon unbleached or whole wheat flour

$^1/_2$ to 1 cup vegetable broth

$^1/_2$ cup shredded cheese (optional)

Wholemeal Crust or Classic No-Dairy Crust (optional)

3 cups cooked mashed potatoes (optional)

Preheat oven to 350°F.

In a large saucepan, heat the olive oil and sauté any combination of the diced vegetables in the oil until tender—the cooked mixture should measure roughly 2 to 3 cups.

To the sautéed vegetables add any or all of the additional vegetables—to measure 1 to 2 cups when cooked (remember, greens will reduce in volume). Cook briefly to wilt greens and heat frozen ingredients through.

Season with parsley, dried herbs, salt and pepper to taste.

Sprinkle mixture with flour. Stir well and simmer for a few minutes to allow flour to cook, then add the vegetable broth, stirring until moist and thickened. At this stage, you may also add the cheese if desired.

Place ingredients in a prepared round deep-dish pie plate. You may use a bottom crust, a top crust, or both (see Wholemeal Crust, page 176, or Classic No-Dairy Crust, page 78; double the recipes for a two-crust pie)—or no crust at all.

If you decide to go crustless, top pie with about 3 cups cooked mashed potatoes (dotted with butter, if you like).

For the final touch, either cut a special symbol in the crust with a sharp knife or a special cookie cutter, or swirl one in the potatoes, using a spatula or spoon (suns or spirals are two great choices). Make your shape with gratitude in your heart for this good food and for the sun's return.

Bake your pie for 45 minutes, or until crust is golden, and serve. (For a grand presentation, surround the pie on its serving platter with fresh evergreens.)

PLUM PUDDING

serves 6 to 8

Dark and rich as the winter earth, plum pudding is the perfect Yuletide dessert, reminiscent of Dickensian holidays and those more ancient still. This is a recipe to begin at dusk and come back to at dawn: you'll want to start preparing it a day ahead of time.

2 cups raisins

1 cup chopped prunes (the plums in plum pudding)

³/₄ cup currants

¹/₂ cup sultanas or golden raisins

1 cup Guinness stout

1 cup unbleached white flour

¹/₂ cup firmly packed brown sugar

¹/₃ cup mixed candied citrus peels

¹/₄ cup finely chopped almonds

¹/₄ teaspoon each:

    Freshly grated nutmeg

    Cinnamon

    Allspice

¹/₄ cup fine, dry bread crumbs

8 tablespoons butter or shortening

2 eggs, lightly beaten

Pinch of salt

In a ceramic bowl, combine the raisins, prunes, currants, sultanas or golden raisins, and Guinness and allow to steep, covered, overnight. (You could do this as part of your Yule Eve ritual. Then, as you sit in your Power Place in the gathering darkness, you can think of these fruits resting quietly in the dark so that they can be a part of your festive Yule celebration when the light returns.)

The next morning, after you greet the newly risen sun, place this Guinness-fruit mixture in a large bowl and combine with the flour, brown sugar, candied citrus peels, chopped almonds, nutmeg, cinnamon, and allspice.

In a smaller bowl, combine the bread crumbs, butter or shortening, eggs, and salt. Add this egg mixture to the ingredients in the large bowl and mix well.

Generously butter a 1½-quart pudding mold or a heat-proof bowl. Spoon batter into mold and cover with lid or buttered aluminum foil tied onto bowl with string.

Place a rack in a deep soup pot with enough hot water to come halfway up the sides of your mold when set on the rack. Steam pudding for around 2 to 2½ hours, allow to cool until just warm, and unmold.

You may decorate and serve your plum pudding in so many magical ways:

Splash with warm brandy and light with a match.

Cover with a doily and sift powdered sugar over it, then remove the doily—
    instant snowy lace! Make a traditional hard sauce and enjoy the contrast of
    dark pudding and snowy sauce.

Surround and/or top your pudding with:

- Fresh greens
- Dried orange rounds—like little suns
- Clean rocks and stones (the earthy darkness of the pudding lends itself beauti-
    fully to honoring the element of earth—build a small cairn around it and top
    with a lighted candle to symbolize the sun's return out of darkness)
- Sprigs of holly
- Favorite holiday ornaments
- Bare winter branches—or a grapevine wreath—laced with either gold ribbon
    or small lit tapers (be watchful).

STORY OF THE LATE WINTER GODDESS

Now the holidays are over and Spring is still so far away. Soon you will feel my seeds stirring beneath the frozen soil—but not yet. Some of you find this waiting time the hardest time of all. Pour yourself a cup of tea and put your feet up. Have I got a story for you.

Once there was a woman who longed to travel. Her little village seemed mean and small in comparison to the great world beyond its gates, and she yearned to pack a bag and set off on a quest for something, anything would do. So great was her longing that she stopped enjoying the beauty of her own little town. The clock that sang a hymn of rejoicing every hour, the shops with their fresh breads and delicious cheeses, even her neighbors ceased to interest her, and the stories they told of their doings and longings made her impatient and even more eager to be gone.

"What have I got in common with anybody here?" she would think. "My destiny is far greater than anything they could ever hope for. The sooner I can get out of here, the better. I'm bored to death."

Now, just as the Winter was nearly—but not quite—over and the woman was beginning to think of packing in earnest, a stranger rode into town, sailing down the icy main street in a black sedan. This stranger had a mane of black hair and wore black stiletto heels. She stopped in front of the house where the woman was making lists of things to take on her trip and beeped her horn. "Wanna lift?" the stranger asked, and the woman was packed and out the door in the time it takes to sneeze. Three miles down the road, the black sedan skidded on a patch of ice, rolled down a steep bank, and flipped over. The woman crawled out of the car just in time to see the stranger in black heels disappear—poof!—and then the car went up in flames. Well. The woman limped back home.

A few days later, another stranger rode into town. This time, her hair was as red as her bright red limo. Once again, the stranger stopped at the woman's door and leaned on the horn. "Going my way?" she hollered, and the woman threw a toothbrush in her bag and flew out the door so fast, the dust mites thought they were having a party.

Five miles down the road, a snowstorm hit, so thick you couldn't see the hood ornament. The stranger, who didn't know this road at all, drove around a bend too fast and crashed right into a stone wall. Just before the limo hit—poof—the stranger was gone. When the woman had untangled herself from the car and crawled onto the road, a neighbor in a battered pickup happened to see her through the snow and stopped to help her. Together they inched home.

In a week or two, when the ice had just begun to melt and a few brave birds had come back to stay, another stranger drove into town in a silver Jeep. She was wearing silver cowboy boots and had a fuzz of silver hair. She stopped the Jeep in front of the woman's house, got out, and knocked on the door. "Do you know where I can get a good cup of coffee?" she asked. Three weeks later, after the woman had taken the stranger to all the best cafes, bought her the town's famous bread and fixed her grilled cheese over the fire the way her mother had taught her, the silver-haired stranger looked out the window at the thawing world and said, "Well, I guess I'll be travellin' on. Thanks a bunch. See ya."

"Now wait just a minute!" cried the woman indignantly, "I've given you a great place to stay and the best meals for miles around for three weeks. You couldn't ask for a nicer little town than this—the people are helpful and the food is terrific. And this is the thanks I get? Aren't you even going to invite me to come along?"

"You make it sound pretty great here. You sure you wanna go?" the silver-haired stranger asked with a twinkle.

Without a second's hesitation, the woman replied emphatically, "You better believe it."

"Just checking," said the stranger and together they rode off in the silver Jeep.

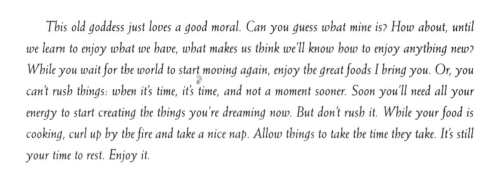

This old goddess just loves a good moral. Can you guess what mine is? How about, until we learn to enjoy what we have, what makes us think we'll know how to enjoy anything new? While you wait for the world to start moving again, enjoy the great foods I bring you. Or, you can't rush things: when it's time, it's time, and not a moment sooner. Soon you'll need all your energy to start creating the things you're dreaming now. But don't rush it. While your food is cooking, curl up by the fire and take a nice nap. Allow things to take the time they take. It's still your time to rest. Enjoy it.

LATE WINTER RECIPES

THOUSAND-NAMES BEAN SOUP

serves 8 or more

They say the Goddess has a thousand names. This soup has a thousand beans (more or less). Think of each beautiful bean—with its perfect, smooth shell and striking speckles or variations in color—as a gift from the Goddess in your soup pot. This substantial, hearty soup will warm you all the way through, even on the coldest, darkest day. And if you buy lots of different bags of dried beans to mix for this recipe, the leftovers look interesting and attractive in glass jars—and, tied with a pretty ribbon, they make great New Year's gifts. (It's supposed to be good luck to eat beans on New Year's Eve. And it's certainly good for you to eat them anytime.)

> **3 cups dried mixed beans**
> **3 tablespoons olive oil**
> **1 large onion, chopped**

3 or 4 garlic cloves

1 medium carrot, cut into ¹/₂-inch chunks

1 stalk celery, tough strings removed, cut into ¹/₂-inch chunks (optional)

8 cups (or more) vegetable broth

2 teaspoons salt

Dried herbs, 1 teaspoon each of one or more of the following
(as desired):

Marjoram

Sage

Rosemary

Thyme

Savory

Basil

Oregano

1 can tomatoes, chopped (optional)

1 or 2 chipotle peppers (optional)

Half-and-half (optional)

The night before you plan to make this soup, place the dried mixed beans in a large bowl. (You may purchase a bag of fancy beans already mixed, or invest in many bags of different beans to make your own—dried beans are inexpensive.) Cover beans with water and soak overnight. (It can be fun to do this on a full-moon night: imagine your beans soaking up all that lunar energy.)

Next morning, drain the water off your beans and you're ready to make your soup.

If you forget to soak your beans the night before, on the day of your soup-making, place the dried mixed beans in enough water to cover and bring to a boil in a large pot. Boil for 3 minutes (three is a magic number), then cover pot, turn off heat, and allow to sit for 2 hours. Then proceed with recipe.

In a very large soup pot, heat the olive oil, and add the onion, garlic, carrot, and celery and sauté until slightly softened.

Add the vegetable broth, beans, salt, and the dried herbs of your choice to the pot (marjoram, sage, rosemary, or thyme are all delicious; savory is supposed to reduce the gassy effects of beans; basil and oregano, along with a can of chopped tomatoes added in the last half hour of cooking, will give your soup a delightful Italian flavor). This recipe can be adjusted in infinite ways to suit your tastes. Toss in 1 or 2 chipotle peppers if you like (they give a wonderful smoky taste as well as some additional heat).

Bring soup to a boil, then reduce heat, cover, and simmer about 2 hours, or until beans are tender, adding more broth if necessary to thin. Adjust seasoning and serve hot. With crusty bread and a salad, you have a meal. (This soup may also be pureed in a blender: remove chilies before blending, if you used them, and puree all or part of the soup, adding half-and-half, if desired, for an extra-creamy version.)

ROOTED WINTER SALADS

Supermarkets offer a bounty of fresh greens, even when the snow lies deep around us. Many of our ancestors weren't so lucky. Although they may have had an abundance of winter roots and legumes, their craving for crisp greens had to be satisfied with cooked cabbage or kale until Spring. We can have the best of both worlds.

Crisp salad greens
Assorted vegetables—choose from:
   Carrots
   Beets

Turnips

Parsnips

Potatoes

Onions

Rutabagas

Sweet potatoes

Lively accents (optional):

   Chopped nuts

   Raisins

   Cinnamon

   Pomander Dressing (page 110)

   Freshly reamed orange or lemon juice

Choose a medley of your favorite vegetables to prepare simply.

Carrots and onions may be grated or minced raw—everything else may be lightly steamed, roasted, baked, or caramelized, or you could use leftover Heartha's Roasted Winter Vegetables (page 93).

On a bed of the freshest, crispest greens you can find, mound any or all of the warm vegetables to invite Winter's grounded, earthy rootedness into our bodies and our homes.

Winter salads often benefit from a touch of citrus, as well. Feel free to ream an orange or a lemon into your favorite salad dressing recipe to add a touch of Yuletide light and sparkle. Or you could use Pomander Dressing (page 110) and add ¼ teaspoon ground cinnamon; root vegetables, citrus, and cinnamon all cuddle up beautifully together in Winter.

Top with a tablespoon or so of chopped nuts, and/or raisins, if you like.

WINTER SUNSET CARROTS

serves 4 to 6

Something about the bright, clear ginger taste of this recipe coupled with the carrots' startling color evokes winter sunsets and reminds us of the precious quality of light in Winter. The days may be short, but the light is so beautiful.

2 tablespoons olive oil

3 to 4 cups carrots, scrubbed and cut into 1/2-inch rounds

1 to 2 tablespoons maple syrup, honey, or brown sugar

**2 to 3 tablespoons freshly squeezed orange juice (or lemon juice, for a
very zesty version)**

**2 teaspoons fresh minced ginger root (or 1 teaspoon dried powdered gin-
ger, or 2 tablespoons crystallized ginger—use more, if you like)**

Salt to taste

In a medium saucepan, heat the olive oil over medium-high heat. Sauté the carrots in heated oil until just crisp-tender. Then add the maple syrup, honey, or brown sugar along with the orange juice. Stir until carrots are coated and mixture has made a nice glaze.

Sprinkle with ginger and salt to taste. Stir to blend flavors and serve warm.

LEEK AND POTATO GRATIN

serves 4 to 6

Leeks and potatoes make delicious winter partners. This hearty classic is especially warming and soul-satisfying, since it starts out white as the surrounding snow, but ends up as round and golden as the slowly strengthening sun.

2 cups lowfat milk

3 large potatoes, scrubbed and sliced into ¼-inch rounds

2 leeks, washed well, white parts only, sliced into ¼-inch rounds

1 garlic clove, minced or pressed

¼ teaspoon salt or more, to taste

1 cup shredded cheese (cheddar is usual, but you could try Gruyère, Jarlsberg, smoked Gouda, or Monterey Jack)

¼ cup grated Parmesan cheese

Preheat oven to 375°F.

In a large heavy-bottomed or nonstick saucepan, combine the lowfat milk, potatoes, garlic, and salt to taste. Simmer over medium heat until potatoes are fork-tender, around 20 minutes: be careful not to scorch.

Using a slotted spoon, transfer leeks and potatoes to a shallow baking dish, retaining the thickened hot milk in your saucepan.

Stir the cheese into the saucepan. Continue stirring until cheese is melted. This dish takes a bit of stirring: you could use your stirring time to think of the snow that will begin to melt in just a little while, and the days that are gradually growing longer.

Pour cheese-milk mixture over leeks and potatoes in baking dish. Sprinkle with Parmesan cheese.

Bake in preheated oven until bubbly and golden, about 30 minutes. Let your gratin cool for about 10 minutes before serving. (This dish is very pretty with a sprig of evergreen on top.)

WINTER FRUIT PIES

makes 4 individual pies, or 1 large pie

Not that long ago, fresh fruit in Winter was an unheard-of luxury for most people. But dried fruits, preserved at the height of Summer with an eye toward the lean winter months ahead, can make delicious desserts with very little trouble. The late winter goddess encourages us to experiment with different combinations, to see what will most please our eyes and palates. The final result is reminiscent of mincemeat pie, but is so much easier—and more healthful—to make.

> **2 cups dried fruit, any combination—choose from:**
>   **Dried figs, prunes, apricots, peaches, pears, or apples—chopped**
>   **Raisins, sultanas, currants, dried blueberries, cranberries, or cherries—halved or left whole**
> **$2/3$ cup brandy, rum, or whiskey**
> **$1/3$ cup firmly packed brown sugar**
> **Juice of one lemon**
> **2 tablespoons butter or margarine**
> **1 teaspoon vanilla extract**
> **$1/2$ teaspoon cinnamon**
> **$1/4$ teaspoon salt**
> **Wholemeal or Classic No-Dairy Crust (optional)**

To make the filling, place 2 cups dried fruit in a medium bowl—you can use any combination that pleases you (my current favorite is $1/2$ cup each apricots, peaches, currants, and raisins).

In a small saucepan, heat the alcohol, brown sugar, lemon juice, butter or margarine, vanilla extract, cinnamon, and salt. Stir over medium-high heat until this sauce bubbles and thickens slightly. Pour over fruit in bowl, stirring to combine. Allow fruit to steep in sauce for at least 15 minutes.

Preheat oven to 375°F.

Meanwhile, roll out dough for your crust of choice. Wholemeal (page 176) or Classic No-Dairy (page 78) Crusts both work well—double the recipe if you plan to make a top crust—or you could save time and use a packaged crust mix or a premade crust.

Cut dough to fit four individual ½-cup tart tins. Press dough lightly into tins, pinching edges decoratively if you wish, and spoon fruits and sauce evenly into crusts. (You may make a lattice top crust or a regular top crust—slashed to allow steam to escape, or decorate the tops with little pastry leaves; or use no top crust at all.)

Bake pies in preheated oven for 35 minutes if you used a top crust, or for 25 to 30 minutes if you didn't (to avoid getting the fruit on top too browned)—until filling is bubbly and crust is golden. Allow pies to cool until just warm before serving.

LAST WORD OF THE WINTER GODDESS

I was just going to take another little nap, but here comes my sister Spring to wake me up. Well, you're probably ready to hear a new story by this time—my children never seem to tire of Spring's return. Just remember that, although you may not think so now, in a few seasons you'll be glad to return to me. When you do, my warm lap will be waiting for you.

Once there was an icicle who thought she was a crystal—singular, beautiful, and motionless—forever unchanging. But one day in early Spring, the Sun whispered a story to her that was so moving, so powerful, that she suddenly remembered: she recalled a time when she had risen and fallen in a graceful dance, part of a great ocean. Remembering this, she became a tear of joy. And so she reentered the dance.

SPRING

S oft breezes freshen the earth, and the world begins to flower. This is the season of renewal; if you need energy and inspiration, think of these magic words:

Spring's watchwords—new, tender, airy, revitalizing, tonic, flowering, lively, fresh, light

Spring scents (that help us spring into a vernal frame of mind)—green onions, dill, vinegar, sweet flowers (hyacinth, lilac, lily of the valley, violet), rain-damp earth

SETTING THE STAGE FOR SPRING

The perfect spring house is perched on a hill. Its eaves are steeped in clouds. Sky peers in through every window. The first rays of dawn turn the slate roof a warm, golden pink. Scores of birds nest in the gables; their lively singing in the morning and the freshness of the wind make it seem as if the house is flying. But that flight is anchored in the quickening earth.

All around the house are freshly dug garden beds, vivid with new shoots and leaves. Fruit trees incline toward the walls, branches starred with blossoms. Fallen petals drift across the door.

Inside, there is a sense of order and spaciousness. When you walk into the kitchen, you notice the clean, fresh feeling there. You stand in the middle of the room, taking a deep breath as you look around at the sunrise colors: pale rose, butter-cup yellow, the tender blue of a wild bird's egg. Someone has polished the floor with loving attention. Someone has cleaned the countertops until they shine.

In the center of the scrubbed wooden table is a pot of flowering paperwhites. Their wild, sweet scent permeates the room. A nest sits nearby, filled with eggs decorated by hand—magical eggs with wishes in them.

The spring house is alive with a sense of the future. In it, plans, dreams, and inspirations can all be planted and nurtured. The door to the outer world is opening. As you look outside at the blossoming earth, your mind fills with hope.

THE SPRING KITCHEN

Spring kitchens are airy, fresh places where we feel stimulated, energized, alive with possibilities. The first step in making our kitchens places of inspiration is a good old-fashioned spring-cleaning. Even those of us who loathe housecleaning as a tiresome, thankless, repetitious, and endlessly boring chore can learn to enjoy the process of marking our territory with magic: see Cleaning (page 10) for some ideas on cleaning with magical consciousness.

By the end of Winter, the world looks a bit scruffy and neglected. Dead leaves and fallen branches litter the ground, along with remnants of snow pocked with grime. Just as a gardener needs to clear away the winter debris to make room for spring growth and flowering, so it can be a good thing to clear away the debris from our kitchens. Make space in your life for fresh, good things to grow. Take some time in early Spring to decide on your kitchen essentials: What is truly necessary for you? What could you do without? Give away anything that doesn't serve you. When your kitchen is clean and uncluttered, your spirit can breathe.

Once your kitchen is as clean as you feel like making it, you may want to celebrate the stirring of new life with a few essential springtime decorations. Flowering bulbs and bare tree branches can both be placed in water and allowed to bloom. Teardrops of glass hung in the window catch the light like melting icicles. Dark, earthy winter colors give way to the lighter, more airy ones of Spring—a pastel rag rug for the floor or a woven mat for the table may refresh your spirit. Look for shades of mouth-watering yellow-green, violet, rose, pale blue, silvery dove-gray, and a tender yellow the color of the emerging sun. These are the colors that will help you to envision, to plan, to be inspired.

Spring is associated with air, and with thoughts, ideas, and words. You could invoke the power of words in your kitchen by writing a few important ones here and there. Use large letters if you want them to be seen (in a border around the ceiling, perhaps), or hide tiny ones in secret places. What are the words that you need in your life? Is there a special quote that you could frame or incorporate into your kitchen?

By the Spring Equinox, the birds are returning and the world is filled with wings, nests, and the heart-lifting sound of their singing. One traditional and pleasant way to commemorate the birds' return is to include a nest or two in your kitchen. You could buy one (Spanish moss, twig, or wicker nests look very realistic), or you could find a real one (as long as it isn't being lived in anymore), or create your own. Although I have a preference for natural materials, you may want to try something completely different: one music-loving friend recycled some ruined audiotape for his spring offering—the shiny brown, curly tape made a perfect nest. And my kitchen Sheela-na-gig appears to enjoy her springtime perch inside an old chiffon scarf.

Fill your nests with eggs. Traditionally, eggs have held a place of special veneration as objects of power and magic. Egg-decorating is an ancient way to honor this season (see Kitchen Rituals for Spring Equinox, page 146, for some ideas). And you may want to tuck in a feather or two, as well—these are especially meaningful if you've found them yourself.

There are egg-shaped soaps available now that would be fun in a nestlike soap dish on the sink (look for nice all-natural herbal egg-soaps in specialty stores or gift catalogs). Or, to make your own, try grating leftover bits of soap into a bowl, mix with a little water, and shape small palmfuls into eggs by hand. If you throw in a few leftover coffee grounds, your soap will have a wild-bird-egg's speckled look and will also be a good deodorizer for oniony hands. Whenever you wash with a bar of egg-soap, let the symbol remind you of the incredible power to create that lies in your hands—and in your heart, your spirit, your mind.

The first tender vegetables of the spring garden make a welcome appearance now. The tiny carrots, cheery radishes, asparagus spears, and the earliest new peas to sprout up in gardens may be found on everything from teapots to vases to dinnerware to teatowels, which will let you invite their hopeful message inside as well. Or you could paint or stencil the veggie of your choice somewhere special: inside a cupboard door to cheer you whenever you open it, for instance.

By late Spring, the world is strewn with flowers. Make a place on your table for a vase spilling over with blooms, or find an O'Keeffe print to brighten your wall. The sensual beauty of flowers has age-old associations with love, sex, and pleasure, and late Spring is certainly the time for those. To invite the power of loving sensuality into your kitchen, choose fabrics and accents in shades of roses to remind you of your own sacred petals. Consider making a rose-patterned pillow for your Power Place; then, every time you sit there, you will be embowered by these rich symbols of the Goddess.

FILM OF THE EARLY SPRING GODDESS

My opening shot shows a dark hillside. It is rounded and bare. You can feel that great mysteries lie beneath its soil—perhaps it is a fairy mound or a place of ancient ritual. The hill is stiff with cold, its dark shape brooding like a sleeping bear against the lightening sky. But when the camera brings you closer, you begin to sense a slight vibration, the pulsing of a faint, fresh new rhythm. Now you move in closer still. You can see inside the mound. Beneath the darkness are the stirrings of life, seeds are swelling, sending out the first pale threads that will help them find

their way out of the dark, out of the winter labyrinth. At the heart of the hill is a
sacred fire, older than your greatest grandmothers. It burns with a clear red flame.
Behind the hill, the sun rises, burning with the same red flame.

Mine is a secret, hidden time. Most of my magic is happening beneath the surface of things,
and that surface is still rigid with snow and ice and barren cold. But when you look more deeply,
you can see that the days are longer. The birds are coming back. The earth is beginning to stir
once again.

Animals, with a wisdom that you human children have forgotten, know that Spring is near.
Now the sleeping ones begin to wake, famished from their long winter sleep. My foods will help
you to waken and be nourished, to bring your energies back out into the world after their long
season underground. You are all my Sleeping Beauties. My season is your wake-up kiss.

SPROUTING MEDITATION

Spring always seems to happen for the first time. Year after year, the endless weeks of
winter cold seem to numb us, to make us forget. Deep inside ourselves, we begin to
believe that it will always be like this—frozen, gray, dead. And then Spring takes us
by surprise. For uncounted centuries, people have paused to celebrate this seasonal
miracle: out of the seemingly barren earth comes new life. From tiny, dead-looking
seeds the first sprouts grow, gladdening our hearts and nourishing our bodies with
their cheerful green.

Sprouts are small emblems of courage and strength—triumphantly bursting out of
their hard, dry coffins, then blindly pushing their way up through cold, dark soil to
find the sun. Even if you live in a big city, you can experience Spring's wonder right
in your own home. Nothing is more amazing, if we take a little time to notice and to
participate.

This is a three-day meditation, but it only takes a minute or two each day, and

those minutes are spent in connection with the outrageously powerful life force that fuels and inspires this planet. If you just don't have the time to do the sprouting part of this meditation, then buy a box of sprouts at the store and skip directly to Embodying the Spring (page 135).

THE SPROUTING EXPERIENCE

First, find a clean widemouthed one-quart jar.

Next, choose some dried, unhulled seeds or beans to sprout. My current favorites are sunflower seeds, but you could choose alfalfa or lentil, radish, garbanzo, wheat berries—or many other kinds. Just be sure that your seeds or beans aren't treated with any chemicals for planting: they should be intended as food.

Measure out about ¼ cup of your seeds or beans. Pour a few into your palm and really look at them. Roll them around with your fingers, really notice their texture. What a bizarre paradox they represent, these dried-up, rock-hard, dead little things, unassuming and uninspired. Do you sometimes feel like this at Winter's end?

Now, place your seeds in the jar. As you do, breathe a wish for the things you would like to come alive and grow in your life. What do you hope for in the Spring? How would you like to manifest your gifts? What qualities would you like to expand in the coming months?

Cover the seeds or beans with warmish water and allow them to soak overnight. Think of them whenever it occurs to you: they are softening in the water now, preparing to expand and break free of their winter prisons.

Next morning, cover the mouth of the jar with a clean nylon stocking or piece of cheesecloth (a rubber band will hold it in place), and turn the jar upside down to drain.

Cover the seeds or beans with water once or twice a day to moisten, draining off the water immediately each time. (Laurel Robertson recommends giving this sprout-water to your houseplants; they need vitamins, too!) Each time you water your seeds, take a minute or two to notice how they are changing. Do you secretly think that this won't work, that your seeds will just sit there and mold? Do you have "sprouting anxiety" ("This may work for everyone else, but it won't work for me")? On the second or third day, look carefully and you will see that your seeds have split their casings. And then the first fine threads will emerge. After two or three days, your seeds *will* sprout.

Give them another day or two to grow. Then find a sunny place to put them for a few hours so they can turn a gorgeous spring green (just be careful to keep your sprouts on the cool side—otherwise they'll spoil). Once they're green and lush, take a minute to really savor their fresh color and lively energy. Then cover your sprouts and refrigerate them. Sprouts are best when used fresh, within just a few days.

EMBODYING THE SPRING

Take one of your sprouts with you to your Power Place. Sit and give it your full attention for a moment. Really notice the exact shade of its green. Does it remind you of anything? Does the color vary from one end to the other? How would you describe the stalk? Is it tender, pale, vibrant? Straight or curly? Some sprouts are hairlike, while others are clearly the beginnings of small plants. How large are the leaves? How are they shaped?

Sniff your sprout thoughtfully. Sprouts often have a delicate sweet scent, like Spring. Just think: this little miracle came from a tiny, dead-looking seed. Imagine all the ideas and projects that could sprout in you, if you encourage them and consciously participate in the process. What would they be? What would you like to begin?

With these thoughts in mind, eat your sprout. Is it tender or crunchy? How does it taste? Some sprouts are slightly spicy or bitter, others are sweet. Imagine that this sprout will inspire you, helping you to envision wonderful new things this Spring, season of new beginnings. Thank the sprout for its gifts.

KITCHEN RITUALS FOR IMBOLC

The Irish climate is milder than ours; to the ancient Celts, February 1 was the first day of Spring. They called it *Imbolc*, from the words for 'ewe's milk' or 'in the belly' (sources differ on this), because pregnant sheep began to lactate at this time. Our Groundhog Day is a leftover from the belief that magical animals come out of hibernation now.

Even in the frozen north, Imbolc can begin to show us the first signs of Spring: the days are growing discernibly longer and there is a new energy in the air. More birds are singing, and a few hardy plants may even be showing their first shoots. But most of the activity happening now is underground. Imbolc celebrates not only the strengthening sun, but the waking of the seeds that are beginning to stir in their dark winter beds.

With six weeks or so of wintry weather still ahead of us, Imbolc rituals in the kitchen become an important affirmation that Spring *is* happening, although most of the movement at this point is out of sight. Try bringing a handful of snow or ice indoors. Place it on the stove—associated with Brigid, the Irish goddess of firecraft (Imbolc is sacred to her)—and watch it as it melts throughout the day. Know that soon the world will thaw.

You could also make a Threshold of Spring for your kitchen; its simple stone shape will echo the ancient Druid dolmens that were symbols of rebirth and renewal. In a pan or plate filled with dirt deep enough to anchor them, place two long rocks, standing up. Place a third rock across the tops of these standing stones—now you have made a threshold or gateway. Imbolc is such a threshold; through it, we can see the first glimmering light of Spring. Place a candle in the middle of your gateway to light at dusk.

Today is the perfect day to gather up and compost or burn any dry, dusty evergreens left over from the Winter Solstice, and to do a little spring-cleaning (see Sue Bender's *Plain and Simple* for some inspiration: there are real spiritual benefits to getting all of your surfaces sparkling). If you're not up to doing the whole kitchen yet, you could do a microcosmic cleaning by dusting your kitchen altar; it counts. And since the oven, a source of fire, is sacred to Brigid, today would be a good time to clean it. Then you may want to light a white (or red-orange) candle inside it to invoke Brigid's presence there.

We can also honor Brigid's flame with the following special festival loaf. This recipe was given to me by Maura D. Shaw, fellow cookbook-writer and dearest friend, who so generously makes the most wonderful foods for every special occasion. This particular version of traditional Irish soda bread can trace its lineage back to the sea-port of Dingle in County Kerry, Ireland, where it was baked over a peat fire.

MAURA'S IRISH SODA BREAD

This cottage loaf has Imbolc magic in it: it is as round as the sun, is filled with sun-colored raisins, and has a sprinkling of caraway seeds to remind us of the seeds that are awakening now. There is something very satisfying about shaping this loaf by hand, an evocation of the days when bread was baked in a peat- or wood-fired oven dedicated to a goddess of the hearth.

$3^{1}/_{2}$ **cups unbleached flour**
$^{1}/_{2}$ **to** $^{3}/_{4}$ **cup raw or brown sugar**
1 teaspoon baking powder
$^{1}/_{4}$ **teaspoon baking soda**
1 stick butter, softened
1 egg
$1^{1}/_{4}$ **cups buttermilk (or regular milk soured with 1 teaspoon vinegar)**
$^{1}/_{2}$ **cup golden raisins or currants**
1 teaspoon dried caraway seeds (optional)

Preheat oven to 350°F.

In a large mixing bowl, combine the flour, raw or brown sugar (use more if you like a sweet loaf), baking powder, and baking soda.

Cut butter into flour mixture until crumbly.

Add the egg and the buttermilk. Mix until moistened. Dough will be stiff. Add, working into dough, the golden raisins or currants and the caraway seeds.

Form into a round loaf on a greased baking sheet. Use a knife to cut a spiral or other pattern into the top, if you wish; sunlike Brigid's crosses are also traditional.

Bake in preheated oven for 1 hour.

EARLY SPRING RECIPES

BRIGID'S BROTH OF INSPIRATION

serves 4 to 6

By the beginning of February many of us, weary of the unending cold and gray, find ourselves suffering from full-blown winter blahs. Imbolc's ancient associations with the first day of Spring are tantalizing, but we know we still have a full month (or more) of cold weather ahead of us. The vista is unappealing. How can we imagine new projects when we feel so low? How can we energize ourselves when we still feel so stuck?

Well, take heart. Irish Brigid (or Bridget, or Brigit, or Bride), the redheaded and fiery goddess of inspiration and healing (among other things) can give us what we need to break out of our hard, dry winter shells. Make her delicious, spicy soup as a wake-up call to your own inner self: the ingredients will give you the courage to face the demands of Spring with renewed zest and vigor.

Before you begin, you may want to invoke Brigid by lighting a small candle near your chopping board. Its warm flame will remind you of her sacred fire.

And you could remember—or say or sing—the following English variation of the ancient Gaelic Blessing of Brigid:

> *I am under the shielding*
> *Of Brigid each day;*
> *I am under the shielding*
> *Of Brigid each night.*
>
> *Brigid is my comrade-woman,*
> *Brigid is my maker of song,*

Brigid is my helping-woman,
*My choicest of women, my guide.**

2 tablespoons olive oil

3 leeks, white parts only, washed well and cut into ¹/₂-inch rounds

1 red bell pepper, diced

1 medium carrot, diced

2 teaspoons paprika

¹/₄ teaspoon (or more) cayenne

6 cups vegetable broth or water

Sea salt to taste

Handful of garlic-mustard greens, coarsely chopped

1 to 2 cups croutons

Sour cream as topping

Sprouts for garnish

In a large soup pot, heat the olive oil. Add the leeks, red pepper, and carrot and heat, stirring occasionally, until barely tender. Sprinkle vegetables with paprika and cayenne to taste. As you sprinkle, visualize Brigid's fiery energy filling the pot; the cheery orange-red color is a warming reminder of her vivid hair, and of the sun that is slowly bringing the frozen earth back to life.

Cover vegetables with vegetable broth or water and sea salt to taste. Bring to a boil and cook, covered, for 15 minutes.

Add the handful of garlic-mustard greens (use a field guide and search your own yard, if possible: garlic mustard is usually up and growing, even at this chilly time of

* This excerpt of the much longer work from *Carmina Gadelica*, by Alexander Carmichael, comes by way of Elizabeth Cunningham, who set it to music for a recent Imbolc celebration.

year). If garlic mustard is not available, substitute parsley or watercress. As you stir these into the broth, think of the green of the new plants just beginning to sprout and grow outdoors. This same green vitality is now a part of your soup.

Continue cooking for 2 or 3 minutes.

Place several croutons into individual bowls, ladle soup into bowls, and top each serving with a dollop of sour cream.

Arrange 2 or 3 of the sprouts from your Sprouting Meditation (page 132) on the sour cream. There you have it: a broth as fiery as Brigid's hair, topped with sprouts emerging from the snow—a warming and reviving homage to Spring's return.

SPROUTED SPRING SALADS

Add some spring vitality to your salads with the sprouts you grew for your Sprouting Meditation—or try some of the sprouted offerings at your local grocery or natural foods store. Any or all of the following sprouts make great additions to your salad bowl:

Adzuki	**Oat**
Alfalfa	**Radish**
Barley	**Soy**
Garbanzo	**Sunflower**
Lentil	**Wheat berry**
Mung	

You may want to dip mung or other sprouted beans in hot or boiling water for a few seconds before rinsing with cold water and adding to your salad. Soybeans need to be boiled for 5 minutes to remove harmful enzymes. (All sprouts contain some saponins, but these are not toxic unless eaten in huge quantities—moderation is the key.)

SPRING GREENS

serves 4 to 6

Next time you're at the grocery store or the local produce market, notice how many different kinds of greens there are. What will you choose for this quintessential spring food? You could use the tender tops of radishes or turnips that many people just throw away, or the succulent leaves of new beets. Spinach, collards, watercress, mustard greens, or bok choy will all work well, too. Or you could forage in your backyard for some early dandelions. You may combine several greens for this recipe, or stick to just one. Either way, you are eating the Earth's green energy when you make this dish in Spring.

6 to 8 cups packed greens
Sea salt, tamari, or shoyu to taste
1 tablespoon chopped scallion or green onion (optional)

Bring a large pot of water to a boil.

Using a steamer basket, steam greens for a few minutes until just tender.

Sprinkle each serving with sea salt, tamari, or shoyu to taste and chopped scallion or green onion if desired.

MAGIC ISLE PASTIES

serves 4

Pasties are main-dish turnovers, like little portable potpies. They are popular in many places: throughout the British Isles, and in the upper peninsula of Michigan (where I was introduced to them). This delicious vegan version is warming, nourishing, and filled with a foretaste of Spring—the perfect Imbolc offering. And, like so many of the recipes in this book, the ingredients may certainly be varied according to your tastes and the contents of your pantry or fridge.

THE EARTH MOTHER'S SEASONS

Pie crust dough (enough for 2 crusts)
2 tablespoons butter or olive oil
1 onion, diced
2 cups chopped cabbage
1 medium potato, diced
1 carrot, diced
$1/2$ green pepper, diced
$1/4$ to 1 cup vegetable broth (the amount needed will vary)
$1/2$ cup chopped wild greens, watercress, or parsley
3 green onions, chopped
Herbs: savory, dill, thyme, sage—whatever sounds good to you
Sea salt and freshly ground black pepper to taste

Preheat oven to 375°F.

In a large saucepan, heat the butter or olive oil. Add the onion, cabbage, potato, carrot, and green pepper and stir frequently until vegetables are softened. Moisten vegetables with a little vegetable broth.

When vegetables are tender, add the wild greens, watercress, or parsley, green onions, herbs, and sea salt and pepper to taste.

Divide crust dough into 4 balls and roll out to form ovals approximately 8 inches by 5 inches. Heap each oval with about $1/2$ cup of the vegetable mixture, then fold long end over and crimp edges together. If you have any leftover filling, bake it in a dish alongside your pasties, or save it to use in soups, stews, or scrambled eggs.

Place pasties on a baking sheet and bake in preheated oven 30 to 40 minutes or until pastry is golden. May be served hot or warm.

WAKING EARTH CAKE

serves 6 to 8

This unusual cake is an adaptation of a recipe from Harriet Kofalk's The Peaceful Cook. *When you read the (very short) list of ingredients, you may wonder how anything this simple could taste good: the cake contains no salt, no vanilla, no butter or eggs. But it is good—not overly sweet, but very satisfying—and molasses offers us a nourishing tonic for the last cold days of early Spring.*

If you include a special surprise* or two in your batter, you can experience a true Imbolc delight: this tasty cake (that looks so like the slumbering earth) is hiding a wonderful gift, just as the earth is gestating the waking seeds and the first stirrings of Spring.

> **1¹/₂ cups whole wheat flour**
> **1 cup unbleached white flour**
> **1¹/₂ teaspoons baking soda**
> **¹/₂ cup vegetable oil**
> **¹/₂ cup unsulphured molasses**
> **¹/₂ cup hot water**
> **¹/₄ cup blackstrap molasses**
> ***Surprises for hiding inside cake (optional):**
>> **Clean coin**
>> **Small polished crystal**
>> **Ring**
>> **Small gold or silver charm**
> **Yogurt or ice cream as topping (optional)**

Preheat oven to 375°F.

In a large bowl, combine both the flours and baking soda. Stir in the vegetable oil and the unsulphured molasses. This mixture will resemble crumb topping. Remove 1 cup of it and reserve.

In a small bowl, combine the hot water and the blackstrap molasses. Add to remaining mixture in large bowl and stir to mix thoroughly.

Now is the time, if you desire, to stir in any one or more of the non-meltable surprises. Finding one of them in your piece of cake is good luck—but be sure to warn your eating audience, to prevent accidental choking or broken teeth!

Pour batter into a buttered 9-inch-square baking pan, sprinkle with reserved crumb topping, and bake in preheated oven until toothpick inserted in center comes out clean.

Serve warm, with a dollop of yogurt or ice cream, if you like. (Vanilla ice cream works beautifully to represent the snow covering this waking earth.) You could also top your cake with lighted candles, one for each person who will be enjoying it.

FILM OF THE MIDSPRING GODDESS

The first scene of my film is all in shades of black and white: bare tree branches, dead grass, metallic gray sky. But watch closely—it is changing as you watch. Can you see the branch-tips beginning to swell?

Keep looking. There are tiny leaf-buds on the trees now: you can see them better as the camera backs up. A wider view shows the world covered with a gauzy veil, reddish purple and yellow-green. I am the goddess of transformations, changing everything with color that moves and grows. My whole spring world is filmed in time-lapse.

Now the buds are opening. Soon the trees will burst into leaf. Already, there are stocky, strong shoots at their feet, with egg-shaped buds that are blooming, even in the cold. Soon the film will move into fast-forward and cherry and plum blossoms will ring out like bells. In a corner of the final frame is one perfect branch, tipped with pale flowers, graceful as a maiden goddess against a background of softening sky.

The Spring Equinox celebrates the return of life to the world. My sister Persephone is back above ground, the Earth Mother is happy, and everything begins to bloom. My animal children give birth: everywhere you look, nests are full of hungry chicks. Tiny furry ones nuzzle close to their mothers. The world, like the foods I offer you, feels very tender and new.

Do you remember tasting something delicious for the first time? That is how I want you to see my season, as one invitation after another to taste and be delighted and inspired. May you plant good things for the future with every meal you enjoy.

KITCHEN RITUALS FOR SPRING EQUINOX

The Spring Equinox, which occurs between March 20 and 23, marks a moment of perfect balance between night and day—but after this, the days will be longer than the nights. Imbolc was the threshold to Spring: now the Spring Equinox grabs our hands and pulls us through, leading us joyously into the growing time of year. Many early Western Europeans called this festival *Ostara*, or *Eostre*, named after a Saxon goddess of Spring—which is where the Easter holiday gets its name. It is a celebration of the Earth's resurrection, the return of life and growth and fertility to the world.

The cultural Easter holiday comes wrapped in all of the Goddess's ancient emblems of fertility and birth: flowers, nests, grass, baby bunnies and chicks—and eggs. Throughout the Easter season, we are practically bombarded with eggs, hard-boiled and confectionery, real and plastic. It can be illuminating to think of the ways in which our ancestors revered the egg as a source of life and a symbol of the Goddess.

Egg-dyeing becomes the perfect kitchen ritual activity for Spring Equinox: there are commercial egg-dyeing kits in every grocery store. Or you might like to try doing it the old-fashioned way (*Celebrating the Great Mother* has a section on coloring eggs with food: onion skins, red cabbage, and beets). If you have some time on your hands, consider buying a pysanky-making kit at your local craft shop. Pysanky eggs are an old Ukrainian tradition (once a magical rite) involving a beeswax resist and dyeing process similar to batik (only on eggshells rather than fabric). You could spend several very satisfying hours surrounded by the sweet smell of beeswax and enjoying the brilliance of the colored dyes. Whichever method you use, take time, as you color your eggs, to give some thought to the projects, plans, and dreams that you would like to incubate.

You could also try making an Egg Talisman: the next time you crack open a raw egg, save the empty shell. On a small piece of paper, write your intentions, plans, or dreams. Then fold it up and place it, along with a small crystal or other sacred object, inside the pieces of shell (it helps if you only have two pieces to deal with). Glue the shell back together, then wrap with colorful tissue paper and keep in a safe place.

In this season of new beginnings, perk yourself up by trying something new in the kitchen: a new food (I tried ume plum vinegar for the first time in the Spring and loved it: this unusual ingredient makes a special appearance in several of the Midspring Recipes), a new cooking gadget, a new recipe. We all tend to get stuck in the same boring old routines. Some inspiring spring newness may be just what you need to shake off the last of the winter blahs.

In our kitchen, we have a flat wicker basket for winter hats and mittens. The day we put the basket away is a ritual celebration of Winter's end and the true arrival of Spring. What sort of kitchen Winter-to-Spring ritual could you invent for yourself? Allow the spring winds of creativity to inspire you.

Because spring is associated with air, today would be a good day to light some dried sage and allow your kitchen to be purified by the sacred smoke. Then sit in your Power Place and write lists, make plans, and begin imagining a healthier, more joyful future for yourself, your family, and the planet.

MIDSPRING RECIPES

UKEMOCHI MISO SOUP

serves 4

The first fragile blossoms of Spring always remind me of exquisite Japanese prints. When we make this delicate and delicious soup, we share the Japanese appreciation of Spring's beauty as we honor the Japanese goddess Ukemochi.

Ukemochi is a goddess of food, all food: everything we eat came from her body. This soup makes use of miso, a protein-rich, concentrated paste made from fermented soybeans; according to tradition, soybeans sprouted from Ukemochi's womb. Miso is a staple of Japanese cooking—look for it in the refrigerator section of your local natural foods store.

This recipe is simplicity itself, but it may be varied in so many ways. Although the paler varieties of miso are the sweetest, you could try using a darker type for a heartier taste. Or you might try boiling a few vegetables—onions, potatoes, carrots, zucchini—in the hot water before adding the miso. Simmer some mushrooms in the soup for a couple of minutes; throw in a handful of chopped greens or soaked dried seaweed (wakame or kombu are delicious); or sprinkle in a little dry sherry, toasted sesame oil, or ume plum vinegar. Some cubed firm tofu would add interesting texture and extra protein. Let your spring cravings be your guides.

> **4 cups water**
> **$1/2$ cup yellow miso**
> **1 tablespoon tamari or shoyu**
> **thinly sliced green onion to garnish**

In a saucepan, heat the water.

Place ½ cup of the hot water in a small mixing bowl and add the miso, stirring to dissolve.

Stir miso mixture into remaining hot water in soup pot and mix well, making sure not to boil. (Boiling destroys beneficial organisms: miso, like yogurt, is rich with them.)

Add the tamari or shoyu, stirring to mix.

Ladle soup into bowls and top each serving with green onion.

SALAD NESTS

This salad is a pretty reminder of the returning birds and the nesting activity everywhere.

Alfalfa sprouts
Green onions or scallions, finely chopped
Whole, blanched almonds
Ume Plum Dressing (below)

For each serving, take a generous handful of alfalfa sprouts and gently form the sprouts into a nestlike shape.

Fill each nest with about 1 tablespoon green onions or scallions. Top onions with several almonds (these look charmingly egglike).

Drizzle nests with Ume Plum Dressing.

UME PLUM DRESSING

serves 4

Japanese ume plum vinegar gives a delicate pink color, piquant salty flavor, and delicious fruity, flowery bouquet to this exceptional dressing. Look for it at your local natural foods store: it's worth every penny.

> **¹⁄₃ cup olive oil**
> **2 tablespoons ume (or umeboshi) plum vinegar**

Combine the olive oil and plum vinegar in a jar with a tightly fitting lid. Put the lid on the jar and shake until dressing is smooth.

NEW POTATOES WITH DILL

serves 4

New potatoes are a springtime tradition. The visual appeal of their lovely pinkish color and egglike shape, as well as their overall deliciousness, makes their appearance in our midspring meals most welcome.

> **2 pounds small red new potatoes**
> **2 tablespoons olive oil**
> **Sea salt to taste**
> **2 tablespoons snipped fresh dill**

Preheat oven to 350°F.

Place potatoes in an 8-inch-square baking dish. Drizzle with half of the olive oil and toss potatoes to coat with oil. Sprinkle with sea salt to taste and drizzle again with the remaining olive oil.

Bake in preheated oven, stirring once or twice to ensure even baking, until potatoes are tender inside and crisp outside—about 1½ hours.

Remove potatoes from oven and sprinkle with dill. Serve hot.

SPRING SUPPER OMELET WITH MUSHROOMS

serves 4

Eggs have been revered as magical symbols and talismans of power for millennia. Virtually every ancient or indigenous culture has made use of the sacred egg—for healing, protection, fertility magic, divination, spell-casting, and more.

As you crack the eggs for this dish, really notice how each yolk mimics the sun. Think of the wonder of eggs that contain new life inside their rigid, dead-looking shells. Give a moment or two to honor your own body's eggs, the perfection of their roundness like small moons, the miraculous journey they make (or once made) inside your body. Honor the Great Mother's ability to make new life. It is good to celebrate eggs.

> **2 tablespoons olive oil**
> **1 cup mushrooms, preferably wild***
> **4 green onions, chopped**
> **2 cloves garlic, minced**
> **Splash of:**
>> **Tamari or shoyu**
>> **Ume plum vinegar**
>> **Toasted sesame oil**

*Wild mushrooms are gradually becoming available in grocery stores and markets. But if your store doesn't carry them, substitute the usual kind. Do not try to pick your own unless you're sure you know what you're doing.

6 eggs

Sea salt and freshly ground pepper

Fresh parsley or watercress sprigs for garnish

In a large frying pan with a lid and a metal handle, heat the olive oil. Add the mushrooms to the pan, stirring frequently, until softened.

Sprinkle mushrooms with the green onions and chopped garlic. Add a splash (if desired) of tamari or shoyu, ume plum vinegar, and/or toasted sesame oil.

In a small bowl, lightly beat together the eggs, sea salt, and pepper.

Distribute vegetables evenly in pan and pour in the eggs. Lower heat, cover pan, and cook eggs until they are completely set. Finish omelet in the broiler for a few minutes to brown the top, if desired.

Loosen omelet by sliding a spatula underneath it. Turn out onto a platter, cut in wedges, and serve. (You may garnish each serving with fresh parsley or sprigs of watercress.)

MAPLE CANDY

makes about 1 pound

In New England, maple sugaring time falls near the Spring Equinox, when the sap begins to move in the trees, bringing them back to life. If you live near a maple syrup farm, consider visiting. When you see the buckets filling, you become a witness to this otherwise invisible mystery.

Real maple syrup isn't cheap, but it is well worth the price. It is a uniquely American taste of springtime: Europeans were introduced to this New World treat by Native Americans, who had been making maple syrup for many, many Springs. Maple syrup is a treat we can feel good about—it doesn't harm the trees and it's packed with calcium and other minerals, a bit healthier for us than refined sugar.

This recipe can be a once-a-year splurge. The process is fascinating, and the result is sheer sensual delight—creamy, sweet, like eating concentrated tree-energy.

Seasonal Easter-candy molds offer an opportunity for fun, and when we realize that bunnies and eggs are fertility symbols sacred to the Goddess, their use takes on an entirely new dimension. (Even Easter lilies have a hidden story: they were once sacred icons of the Goddess's vulva. Perhaps it isn't so strange that many Sheela-na-gigs are found in churches.)

2 cups real maple syrup

Use a candy thermometer.

In a sturdy saucepan with high sides, bring maple syrup (the real thing, not imitation) to a boil.

Turn heat to very low and allow to boil without stirring until thermometer reads 233°F. Be careful that the syrup doesn't boil over—once maple syrup finally decides to boil, it *really* boils. The boiling action is mesmerizing; the syrup's dark earthy color in such constant motion reminds us that the earth is constantly moving and changing, even when it appears to remain the same.

When the reduced syrup has reached 233°F, remove it from the heat and allow to cool, still without stirring it, until thermometer reads 110°F.

Now it's time to beat the reduced syrup with a wooden spoon. Beat vigorously for several minutes. (It can help to sing while you do this.) You are making a transformation take place: as you beat, the syrup gradually turns a pale caramel color and it becomes stiff enough to hold a shape.

Place in candy molds or form into patties on a plate or baking sheet and allow to cool completely.

Unmold and enjoy.

FILM OF THE LATE SPRING GODDESS

My film is explicit, sensual, and alive—your culture could even call it X-rated. But to me there is nothing more beautiful in the world than ecstasy. So, my film begins with a garden close-up: flowers blooming, flowers that are clearly the sexual parts of plants. Everything is opening, blossoming without end. I have licked and stroked the world into readiness. Inside each blossom is the seed of Summer's fruit.

My film has a heady fragrance. Even if you close your eyes, the scent of apple blossom, rose, and lilac will wind its way into your soul. Open your eyes: you may catch a glimpse of bright, effervescent energy darting around the edges of the garden. Your kind has long believed in fairies. This is their time.

At the garden's heart is a Maypole. There are human dancers around it, each holding a brightly colored ribbon. The dance is ebbing and flowing, rising and falling, gradually covering the pole with a shining cloak of ribbon. You humans have a place in my erotic dance of life.

Now the camera pulls back. We see the dancers lying, happy and laughing, on the grass. They are feeding each other. As we leave the garden, the last thing we hear is the sound of laughter.

My foods are meant to arouse you—not only to acts of love and sexual pleasure, but to a greater sense of aliveness. It is good to be alive and to have a body. I want to feed your body in ways that celebrate your spirit, your precious life.

Many of my children feel sad at this time of year—it can be depressing to be out of sync with the blooming, ecstatic spirit of my season, or to be alone when everything around you is mating. But my foods will help you to get back in touch with the energies of May. And my planet is waiting to be your lover.

KITCHEN RITUALS FOR BELTANE

It can be hard not to think about sex in the Spring—everything seems to be doing it. Our ancestors had a special festival on May 1 to honor sensual pleasure and the reproduction that is so often its end result. It was called Beltane and it celebrated the amazing fecundity of the Earth and everything that lives upon her.

Beltane is the time of blooming—your kitchen goddess may appreciate a flower on her altar today. Many of our ancestors placed representations of sex organs on their altars at Beltane; a red flower will celebrate the female, or you could make a vulva out of clay or paint one on paper. If you want to include a male organ, appropriately shaped rocks (sometimes called lingams) could be used—or you could make something more graphic out of clay. If you have a partner of the opposite sex, the more subtle among you could use a bell (male clapper inside female shell) to symbolize the union of the sexes. The more obvious could find, draw, or make something visibly erotic.

If you ever thought about making love in the kitchen (with a partner or by yourself), today is definitely the day. You will never look at your kitchen floor (or table or countertop) the same way again.

But the best way to honor Beltane in our kitchens is by cooking sensual foods. Because, whether we live alone or with a loving partner, whether we are sexually active or celibate, we all have bodies. And our wise bodies, with their incredibly complex world of nerve endings and processes, have such an amazing capacity for enjoyment. When we give ourselves foods rich in taste, texture, and visual beauty to feast upon, we feed our spirits and we honor the gifts of Earth.

LATE SPRING RECIPES

SENSUOUS SPINACH SOUP

serves 4 to 6

This simple, delicious, and pretty bright green soup has a sensuous texture that most of us associate with butter and cream—but this vegan recipe achieves the creaminess without the fat, and with a minimum of preparation (more time to stroll around picking wild greens for the Wild Salad, below).

6 cups water or vegetable broth
1 large onion, coarsely chopped
3 potatoes, cut into chunks
1 tablespoon tamari
4 cups tightly packed fresh spinach
2 teaspoons dried basil
Freshly ground black pepper to taste
Salt to taste
Garnishes (optional):
Carrot
Hard-boiled egg
Ground coriander

In a large soup pot, place the water or vegetable broth, chopped onion, potatoes, and tamari. Bring to a boil, then reduce heat, cover, and simmer for 35 minutes.

Add the spinach, basil (a great love herb), and pepper to taste. Cook for another 2 minutes, to wilt spinach.

Remove from heat, and puree soup in batches in a blender. Add salt to taste and serve.

If you've made this soup for a love partner (actual or potential), you may want to garnish with a traditional aphrodisiac. Try either a curl of carrot (use your vegetable peeler) or a slice of hard-boiled egg (with or without a sprinkling of ground coriander on top).

WILD SALAD

On a warm spring day, the call of the outdoors is irresistible. Why fight it? Find some free time, grab a gathering-basket and a good field guide to weeds, and head outside. You are about to experience the ancient pleasure of food gathering. There is no fresher or more healthful food than that which we pick ourselves, and the act of finding and gathering it gives us a bone-deep feeling of satisfaction, a direct link with our gatherer ancestors.

But first, a few cautions:

- *Be sure any yard or wild area you harvest is free from pesticides or other harmful chemicals.*
- *Make sure anything you pick is at least three feet from the road or highway (anything too close to the street will be contaminated by car exhaust).*
- *Avoid areas frequented by dogs, or places where you see animal droppings.*
- *Refer to your field guide—you'll want to be sure you know what you're picking.*

With those warnings out of the way, take a moment to breathe deeply. Close your eyes and lift your face to the sun. Feel the warmth on your closed eyelids. Become aware of your feet, resting firmly on the Earth. Now open your eyes. As you look around, know that you are surrounded by an amazing treasure trove of delicious green food. It isn't wrapped in plastic. It doesn't cost a thing. The Earth Mother offers it to you for free, because you are her child.

Become a treasure seeker—the greens and weeds around you are filled with healing. Begin to wander, looking here and there. When you find something good, pick a little of it and pop it into your basket. Soon, your rhythms will slow, your mind will grow quiet, and at the end of a pleasant ramble in the sun you will have a salad bursting with nourishment and wild goodness.

Greens and weeds you'll want to look for:

Chickweed

Dandelion—both the tender leaves and blossoms

Dock—curly and other varieties

Garlic mustard

Lamb's-quarters

Plantain

Purslane

Red clover

Sheep sorrel

Winter cress or rocket

Wood sorrel

Violet (*Caution:* pick only if you see the exquisite purple flowers; there are a few toxic plants with similar heart-shaped leaves. Once you're sure it's violet, you can use both flowers and leaves.)

What you'll want to have on hand:

Olive oil

Good-quality vinegar or freshly squeezed lemon juice

Head home when you have enough for the people you are feeding. You may want to wash the greens by dunking them briefly in a sink full of cold water, patting them dry

with a clean towel, or you could leave them as is. Toss your greens in a bowl with just a little olive oil and a few drops of good vinegar or freshly squeezed lemon juice. Sprinkle the top with some of the dandelion or violet flowers you found, and serve.

As you savor each tender, delicious mouthful, thank the Great Mother for your Wild Salad experience.

BELTANE ASPARAGUS

serves 4

Fresh asparagus is one of the true pleasures of Spring. These green delights, reminiscent of the male sexual organ, have been prized for centuries as an aphrodisiac. Asparagus has its place in ancient ritual, as well: ancient Greek Maenads rigged up great phallic wands with asparaguslike tips in honor of the power of fertilization.

This Beltane recipe pairs the masculine and the feminine, partnering asparagus with almonds (our ancestors recognized the almond's vulva-shape). This savory method of roasting the almonds comes from my friend Pangea, whose exquisite pottery and delicious food are always an inspiration.

> **1 pound fresh asparagus spears**
> **2 tablespoons butter for sautéing (optional)**
> **Toasted Tamari Almonds (below)**

Wash the asparagus and prepare by snapping off the bottom of each spear with your hands: it will break off with a satisfying crack just at the point where the stem is beginning to turn tough and woody. (Very young, tender asparagus won't need this treatment.)

Steam over boiling water in a steamer basket, or sauté in butter over medium-high heat, for just a few minutes. Asparagus should be bright green and crisp-tender. Place asparagus spears decoratively on plates, tying each "bundle" with a chive, if you like.

Top each bundle with Toasted Tamari Almonds, below.

TOASTED TAMARI ALMONDS

¹/₂ cup sliced almonds
Tamari or shoyu
Butter or olive oil

Preheat oven to 300°F.

Spread sliced almonds in a shallow layer on a baking sheet and sprinkle with Tamari or shoyu and stir to moisten. Dot with butter or a little olive oil.

Bake the almonds, stirring often, for 10 minutes or so, keeping an eye on them, as nuts burn easily. They will smell toasty and delicious when they're done, and they will have turned a rich and delicious golden brown. Make extra if you like, so you can snack on these as you cook—they are highly addictive and delicious.

RISOTTO PRIMAVERA

serves 4

This delicious recipe is bursting with colors and springtime tastes. Think of Botticelli's famous Primavera *painting as you chop and stir—both the painting and this sensually satisfying dish celebrate the pleasures of Spring. It is important to use Arborio rice, a special variety that produces risotto's luscious creaminess.*

1 tablespoon olive oil
1 medium red onion, chopped
1 red bell pepper, seeded and diced
2 cups mushrooms, thickly sliced (you may use button mushrooms
     or a combination of varieties)
2 garlic cloves, minced
1¹/₂ cups Arborio rice

4 cups vegetable stock or water

4 tablespoons chopped fresh parsley

1/2 teaspoon sea salt, or to taste

13 asparagus spears, washed and cut into 1-inch pieces (one spear
for each moon of the year)

1/4 cup grated Romano or Parmesan cheese (optional)

In a large saucepan, heat the olive oil. Add red onion, pepper, mushrooms, and minced garlic. Cook, stirring frequently, for 8 minutes.

Stir in the rice, 2 cups of the vegetable stock or water, the parsley, and sea salt. Bring to a simmer, then cook over low heat, uncovered, for about 10 minutes, stirring frequently.

Stir in the remaining 2 cups of vegetable stock or water and the asparagus. Continue to cook, stirring, until rice is tender, about 10 minutes.

Remove risotto from heat and, if desired, fold in the grated cheese. Serve hot.

You could experiment with different vegetables for this dish: broccoli rabe, spinach, or garden peas could all be substituted for the asparagus.

APHRODITE'S LOVE CAKES

makes about 1 dozen, depending on size

A lot of love-magic starts in the kitchen: sensual meals are often preludes to other sensual pleasures. Here, sweet little cakes blessed by the Greek goddess of love may inspire you to create some special tenderness in the bedroom. Share them with your partner or, if you are solo, have a few as a preface to some self-loving pleasure. Either way, these cakes will help to get you in the mood.

¹/₄ cup whiskey or brandy

2 tablespoons dried damiana (a potent aphrodisiac herb; if your local natural foods store doesn't carry it, see Supplies)

2 tablespoons dried rose petals, crushed

¹/₂ cup whole wheat flour

¹/₂ cup unbleached white flour

¹/₂ cup rolled oats (oats are a great sexual tonic: the phrase, "Sow your wild oats" has a basis in fact)

2 teaspoons baking powder

¹/₂ teaspoon salt

¹/₂ teaspoon ground cinnamon

1 egg

¹/₂ cup honey (honey has long been sacred to the Goddess: here, it reminds us of the sweetness of love)

¹/₄ cup oil or melted butter

1 teaspoon vanilla extract

Dried coriander

Preheat oven to 350°F.

In a small bowl, place the whiskey or brandy, damiana, and rose petals. Steep this mixture for at least 15 minutes.

In a large mixing bowl, combine both flours, the oats, baking powder, salt, and ground cinnamon.

In a separate bowl, lightly beat the egg. Add the honey, oil or melted butter, and vanilla to the egg and stir to combine.

Now add both bowls of wet ingredients to the dry ones in the large bowl and mix thoroughly.

Grease a baking sheet (you may want to draw magical—or erotic—patterns in the oil with your finger). Drop dough by tablespoonfuls onto the greased sheet, then sprinkle cakes with dried coriander (traditional for both love and lust). You may want to light a stick of sweet-smelling incense and blow a little smoke over the cakes before you pop them in the oven.

Bake in preheated oven for 10 to 12 minutes or until lightly browned. Honey burns easily, so be careful not to overbake. Cakes will be soft, moist, and chewy.

LAST WORD OF THE SPRING GODDESS

My sister Summer has been busily pushing her way out of the blossoms for weeks. Now she is free and dancing beside me—and you will have to wait nearly a year to see my tender montage again. When I come back to you, you will remember—but you will still be surprised.

My scenes are like gauze or chiffon—delicate, subtle things that flutter and drift, sheer, fleeting, and ephemeral. If Summer had her own film, it would be filled with shots of zucchini blowing up like balloons at a child's party. As you move into my sister's unsubtle season, hold this final shot in your mind:

> *A golden zucchini blossom flares out from the vine like a trumpet announcing a birth. The flower crumples and fades, but at its base is a triumphant green swelling, a pregnant belly that will ripen, in time, into food for your bodies and souls.*

SUMMER

Everything blooms and ripens now. It is the time of greatest light and warmth. To celebrate this exuberant season, call on these summer words:

Summer's watchwords—abundant, fiery, fresh, fruity, hot, juicy, rich, ripe, succulent, opulent

Summer scents (smelling any of these on even the snowiest winter day is guaranteed to evoke summer and summer energies)—freshly cut cucumbers, food cooking on a grill, watermelon, crushed mint, the mouth-watering tang of lemons and limes, new-mown grass, fresh basil

SETTING THE STAGE FOR SUMMER

The perfect summer house is ringed with shady trees and tangled flowerbeds. It is an easy dance from the garden to the kitchen—you saunter inside, hips swaying, your basket heavy with edible treasure. When you set the basket down, you stretch lazily, pausing for a moment to luxuriate in the vivid colors all around you, the sunshine blazing everywhere.

Wide French doors open out onto a terrace blooming with flowers and herbs in big terracotta pots. Scarlet tiles feel cool under your bare feet, and the wood-fired brick oven burns only in the early morning, before the day heats up—but its smoky scent follows you as you move from table to cupboard. You pause at the alcove in the wall, where a statue of the Grain Goddess sits smiling, a sheaf of wheat in her hand.

Beyond the windows, a landscape lush with green unfolds, fruits and vegetables shining like brightly colored jewels among the leaves. Indoors, bowls and baskets overflow with fresh foods—eggplants in their glossy purple glory, peppers in vivid hues of red and yellow and green, tomatoes sizzling with color and pungent scent, ears of corn with hair as silky and abundant as the Goddess's own. Melons, fruits, and berries, like little pregnant bellies, fill the kitchen with a fragrance sweet as honey, and your eyes close blissfully as the scent of fresh herbs wafts around you—dusty sage, shiny succulent basil, crisp thyme, pungent rosemary.

You can feel a passion for life lighting your body and spirit like flame. As you begin preparing your evening meal—as you choose and chop and stir and taste—you realize that the act of cooking has become your joyous dance.

THE SUMMER KITCHEN

Decorating the summer kitchen can be an exercise in having a little wild fun. Summer colors and shapes make us feel as vibrant and bountiful as this glorious season and can be used to encourage the growth and fulfillment of wishes, plans, or projects in many ways.

If you would like to feel more prosperous or fertile, you can align yourself with Summer's energies by choosing to decorate your kitchen with green—leaf green, moss green, grass green—the color of growing things. Renew a tired kitchen chair with a coat of green paint, or find some old green tiles to make a backsplash for your sink. Paper leaves are fun to strew around the room in various ways, or you could paint leaves on any available surface, if you're artistically inclined. And green potted plants add their encouraging presence to your countertops or table.

For more confidence, warmth, or success, choose fiery red, sunny yellow, rich, buttery amber or goldenrod, mouth-watering tangerine. Sun-colors have been associated for centuries with the oomph it takes to make things happen. Paint a big golden sun above your stove, or experiment with vivid rag rugs or hot-colored dinnerware.

And it's easy to make a connection with nature's abundant energy by picking a little wild beauty to honor in your kitchen—the Earth is blooming in a thousand ways just outside your door. From the simple (a handful of dandelions or long grass plopped in a jar) to the more complex (fragrant blooms from the garden or a roadside patch of weeds, tendrils of berry-covered brambles, a bowl of ripe, dewy fruit), summer decorations are an evocation of bounty, richness, delight, and nourishment. By honoring the loveliness growing all around us, we invite Summer's positive energies into our home.

As the Summer begins to wane after August 1, you may want to include the colors of wheat and golden corn in your decorations. Braided wheat figures or a wreath made of corn husks, or even a bunch of wheat-colored dried grasses for your table, are all beautiful ways to honor the Earth Mother's generosity to her children. See yourself as her representative. Every time you make a meal, you are echoing that Goddesslike power to nourish both body and spirit.

Summer offers so many delights for the eye, the tastebuds, and the soul! But most of us would rather dance and play outside rather than stir and chop and bake indoors for hours in the heat—and so the summer goddesses give us recipes that are simple and easy to prepare. Several dishes are meant to be cooked and eaten outdoors, surrounded by the chirping of insects and the trees' cooling green. Summer teaches us to relax and bask in the security of Earth's bounty: what we need will be given to us. And Summer's gifts are abundantly rich with flavor and color—every bite bursts in our mouths like fireworks that fill our bodies with vitality.

DANCE OF THE EARLY SUMMER GODDESS

My curves are luscious. My hair is thick and braided with corn stalks and the long, pliant green of wild grasses. Dance with me, barefooted—feel the earth warm and alive beneath us. The sun, high overhead, makes our hair shine with haloes. Watch with me as the world ripens and reaches its peak. The hard green fruit-buds of Spring are soft now, fragrant with juice. The young birds are flying and gathering their own food. The foxes have begun to hunt.

What do you hunger for? You have only to ask and I will give it to you.

Early Summer is such a sensual time! Find an hour or two to lie on my warm earth and breathe the scents from herbs and flowers all around you. Or take a walk in the woods and notice how the fragrance changes with every step you take. Allow yourself to open to me and I will show you wonders. This fruitful planet of ours is such a living miracle. I long for you to enjoy it with all your senses, with all your heart.

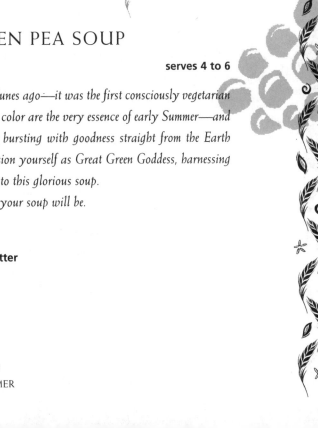

EARLY SUMMER RECIPES

GODDESS'S GREEN PEA SOUP

serves 4 to 6

I discovered this unusual, delightful soup many, many Junes ago—it was the first consciously vegetarian dish I ever made. The delicate flavor and beautiful green color are the very essence of early Summer—and such a lovely surprise. The nourishing ingredients are bursting with goodness straight from the Earth Mother. As you push those buttons on the blender, envision yourself as Great Green Goddess, harnessing the power of the volt to turn little round green goodies into this glorious soup.

The fresher the peas you can find, the more vibrant your soup will be.

> **2 cups hot water**
> **1 cup cashews or ¹/₃ cup cashew butter**
> **¹/₄ cup chopped onion**
> **1 tablespoon olive oil**
> **1 teaspoon salt**

1 garlic clove
1 pound fresh (or frozen) tender green peas
Sprigs of fresh mint for garnish

In a blender or food processor, blend the hot water, cashews or cashew butter, chopped onion, olive oil, salt, and garlic until smooth.

Add the green peas and continue to blend until smooth.

Transfer to saucepan. Thin to desired consistency with added hot water, and heat over medium flame, stirring often, until soup is heated through. Serve immediately or chill for a minimum of two hours and serve cold. This soup is especially pleasing when served with a sprig of fresh mint in each bowl.

FLOWERING SALAD

This lovely salad, like the flowering Earth around us in early Summer, delights the inner artist in all of us: succulent greens starred with colorful blossoms make a feast for both eye and palate.

Use the freshest ingredients you can get your hands on. If you don't have a garden, explore your local farmer's market or produce stand—nothing beats the refreshing coolness of a just-picked cucumber, or the tenderness of young lettuce. Tart wood sorrel adds a delightful lemony note, and edible flowers nourish our spirits with their beauty.

Lettuce leaves for salad base
Cucumber
Sprigs of fresh-picked wood sorrel (or 1 small tomato)
A sprinkle of edible flower heads (try nasturtium—peppery and
        vivid; cucumberlike borage; or calendula)
Salt and pepper to taste
Simple Summer Dressing (optional; below)

For each serving, you'll need a few tender lettuce leaves to use as the base for your salad. Experiment with unusual varieties—many supermarkets now carry organic mesclun or field greens mixtures that are flavorful and rich in nutrients, or you could use curly or red lettuces mixed with the darker green of young spinach. Arrange the greens artfully on a plate.

Take the cucumber and peel it if it's not organic, and cut into either chunks, 1/4-inch rounds, half-moons, or long quarters.

Place cucumber pieces on top of the bed of lettuce, along with several sprigs of fresh-picked wood sorrel. (This plentiful wild green is available in most yards at this time of year: just be sure to avoid sprayed or contaminated areas. Look for their cloverlike leaves and tiny white or yellow flowers. If wood-sorrel is unavailable, substitute one small ripe tomato, cored and cut into quarters or chunks.

Decorate each salad with the flower heads. Dust this salad with salt and pepper to taste, and drizzle with Simple Summer Dressing if desired.

SIMPLE SUMMER DRESSING

enough for 4 servings

1/3 cup extra-virgin olive oil
2 tablespoons red wine vinegar or freshly squeezed lemon juice
1 garlic clove, crushed
Sea salt to taste
Freshly ground black pepper to taste

Combine the ingredients and whisk until smooth.

DAYLILY-BUD SAUTÉ

This scrumptious food was introduced to my family one glorious Summer Solstice by Raven, weed-woman and friend. I had long been an admirer of beautiful daylily flowers, but I never knew you could eat them. What a concept! And such a simple dish—who ever said that recipes had to be complicated and time-consuming to be delicious? Daylily-Bud Sauté goes from gathering-basket to table in minutes and is rich with the Earth Mother's wildness.

Daylilies are a glorious sign that Summer has unfolded around us. Their brilliant orange trumpets, which bloom for only a single day before they curl and fade, remind us to truly enjoy our planet's gifts in the moment. We open our hands to the Earth Mother's bounty when we delight, not only in the sight of the daylily's bright flower, but in the taste and nourishment it offers.

Fresh daylily buds can usually be found in profusion all over—in your own yard or just around the corner. Pick only the firm unopened buds, and be sure that no sprays or chemicals were used wherever you find them.

1 handful daylily buds per serving
1 to 2 tablespoons olive oil
Sea salt or tamari, to taste
1 garlic clove, crushed (optional)
1 tablespoon chopped onion (optional)

Gather a handful of buds for each serving you wish to make.

Sauté the buds over medium-high heat in 1 to 2 tablespoons olive oil. Season to taste with sea salt or tamari. Throw in a clove of crushed garlic, if you wish, or a tablespoon or so of chopped onion for each serving. Enjoy every marvelous bite.

JUNO'S SUMMER QUICHE

serves 4 to 6

This quiche celebrates the Roman goddess who gave us the name for the month of June. Juno, once revered as an omnipotent goddess of female power, was gradually diminished by the patriarchy until she became merely the jealous, shrewish wife of the god Jupiter. But we know the real story! Her quiche is stuffed with fresh summer goodies that will help you to feel as strong and powerful as Juno in her prime. Tomatoes—both sundried and fresh—and sprigs of rosemary, added to the glories of fresh garden vegetables, give this quiche a Mediterranean flair that Juno doubtless would have enjoyed.

2 tablespoons olive oil

1 medium onion, thinly sliced

2 garlic cloves, crushed

2 cups fresh spinach, coarsely chopped

$^1/_2$ cup julienned red bell pepper strips

$^1/_3$ cup oil-packed sundried tomatoes, chopped

1 Wholemeal Crust (below)

2 cups grated cheese, all one kind or a mixture—Gruyère is the
    best, but Jarlsberg or Swiss are fine, and some Monterey Jack
    or cheddar could be thrown in if you're short of the other
    kinds (reduce the fat in this dish by using lowfat or nonfat
    cheeses)

3 tablespoons grated Parmesan or Romano cheese

1 tablespoon whole wheat flour

2 dashes sea salt

2 or 3 eggs

$1^1/_2$ cups lowfat milk

1 medium tomato, thinly sliced

Fresh rosemary sprigs for garnish

White pepper to taste

Preheat oven to 375°F.

In your favorite saucepan, heat the olive oil over medium-high heat. Add the onion and garlic, stirring frequently until vegetables are barely tender. Then add the spinach, pepper strips, and chopped sundried tomatoes. Continue cooking for several minutes longer.

Spread vegetables evenly over an unbaked bottom crust in a 9-inch pie plate (see Wholemeal Crust recipe, below). Or, for an even more pronounced Roman flavor, you could make a simple polenta as the base for this quiche—try one of the excellent boxed mixes available nearly everywhere.

Sprinkle over the vegetables the grated cheese of your choice along with the grated Parmesan or Romano cheese, flour, and a dash of sea salt.

In a small bowl, whisk together the eggs, lowfat milk, and dash of sea salt until smooth and pour the resulting custard over the vegetables and cheese. Place tomato slices decoratively on top of the quiche, along with several fresh sprigs of rosemary. Grate some white pepper over it all, in honor of Juno's notoriously peppery temper.

Pop the quiche into your preheated oven and bake for 40 to 45 minutes until puffy, fragrant, and golden brown. Enjoy the beauty of your creation.

WHOLEMEAL CRUST

enough for one 9-inch pie bottom

This delicate crust makes an excellent base for both quiches and sweet pies.

¹/₂ cup whole wheat or graham flour
¹/₂ cup unbleached white flour
Dash of sea salt

¹/₃ cup chilled butter, cut into small pieces

2 to 3 tablespoons ice water

Combine the whole wheat or graham flour, white flour, and dash of sea salt in a bowl.

Using a pastry cutter or two knives, mix in the chilled butter pieces. Continue to blend, rubbing the dough with your fingers if necessary, until mixture resembles coarse meal.

Add 2 to 3 tablespoons ice water and mix with your hands until the dough forms a ball.

Dust your surface with flour and roll out the dough until it is a flat circle one inch larger than your pie plate. Place it in the plate, pinching the edges decoratively if you wish. Then fill and bake as directed.

SIMPLE STRAWBERRY SHORTCAKE

serves 6

Simple is good. At my favorite strawberry festival, held each year along the Hudson River in Beacon, New York, you can listen to some great old-fashioned folk-singing while you stuff yourself with a quintessential, simple strawberry shortcake that absolutely melts in your mouth—my idea of the perfect summer experience.

Ideally, we should all be able to go out to our garden, or a pick-your-own farm down the road, and gather a basketful of fragrant strawberries, luscious with juice and flavor (the very thought makes my mouth water). But even the strawberries we buy at the grocery store are summer-wonderful, little evocations of the Goddess in all her scarlet glory. Either way, strawberries with Whole Wheat Shortcake Squares are a healthy, delectable tribute to Summer, wherever you live.

WHOLE WHEAT SHORTCAKE SQUARES

Not only is this version a lot healthier than the classic fat-laden shortcake, it is also much quicker to make: no rolling-out is necessary. (More time to play!)

2 cups whole wheat flour
2 tablespoons brown sugar
1 tablespoon baking powder
1 teaspoon baking soda
¹/₂ teaspoon cinnamon
¹/₄ teaspoon salt
¹/₂ cup milk, buttermilk, or soy milk
2 tablespoons vegetable oil
Fresh strawberries, sliced, as desired
Whipped cream or yogurt, as desired

Preheat oven to 450°F.

In a mixing bowl, combine the whole wheat flour, brown sugar, baking powder, baking soda, cinnamon, and salt.

Stir vegetable oil and either milk, buttermilk, or soy milk into flour mixture with a fork until moistened. Mixture will be sticky. Spread the dough in a lightly greased 8-inch-square baking pan.

Bake in preheated oven for 10 to 15 minutes, until lightly browned. Cool for five minutes.

To serve, cut shortcake into 6 pieces. Split each piece and stuff with sliced fresh strawberries—and yogurt or whipped cream, if you like—then put more strawberries and whipped cream or yogurt on top. You have created a dessert fit for a goddess.

DANCE OF THE MIDSUMMER GODDESS

Some of my children in Africa called me Litha and honored me at the time of the sun's peak power. My grace still dances with the herds and rises with the green stalks and flowering vines that give my people beans, yams, squash. On the longest day of the year, my radiant disc beats like a drum, reminding you to shine warmly on each other, to nourish yourselves and your children with vivid flavors and colors.

And, believe me, I am one Hot Mama! Strong and tasty as a peeled onion, my power can make your mouth—and your eyes—water. I am blazing with bright colors. My skirts are flames, embroidered with chili peppers and vines heavy with fruit. My Carmen Miranda hat is a cornucopia overflowing with tomatoes and zucchini and luscious purple eggplant. When I dance, the world applauds in amazement.

Look around you, my children. My abundance is everywhere. Do you need something? Take it! I am brimming with beauty and vitamins and sensual pleasures. Celebrate the smooth and sexy shape of a cucumber. Or revel in the petals of a full-blown rose. Enjoy your nakedness that echoes these fruits of my fertile soil. Sniff the smell your skin gives off when you've been in the sun. Now stroke the sweet cheek of a peach or a newborn baby. Celebrate my bountiful gifts through your own perfect, sacred bodies.

TASTY MIDSUMMER RECIPE-MEDITATION

Find a big yellow onion. Set it out in the sun for an hour or so and then pick it up in your hand. Feel its warmth. Stroke its breastlike shape. Close your eyes and take a long, lingering sniff. Now, eyes open, slowly peel off its outer skin. Really notice the papery dryness as it is sloughed off, and the dewy freshness of the layers beneath.

Hold the onion to your lips and savor its warm, smooth kiss. Now get out your trusty wooden chopping board and a good knife. Chop your onion slowly and carefully. Notice how your knife invokes the juice. Can you stand the onion's sudden pungency? Are your eyes streaming?

Heat a saucepan and a tablespoon of olive oil and add your chopped onion. Sauté it slowly, enjoying the roundness of the pan, like a little hot sun in your kitchen, magically changing your onion from hard, opaque, and white to soft, translucent, and golden. Add some cayenne (as much as you can stand!), and watch the colors changing as you stir. Your pan is now sizzling with sun-energy.

Toast a slice of good fresh bread and spread it with your sautéed onions and cayenne. As you savor the strong, hot flavors, think about your inner fire. We have sun-power inside us, too—power to make things change. Fire makes us feel zesty and energized. A mouthful of cayenne can make the stodgiest of us yelp and run for water. A spirit full of fire can change the stuff around us that needs changing. How will you use your fire? What are the fruits of your life right now? What are you creating? Whether it is a peaceful, loving home, a garden, or a quiet spot in the shade for loved ones to rest and feel recharged; whether it is a book, a play, a symphony, or a painting that wraps an entire wall in movement and color; whether you are creating a community, a special friendship, an altar under the trees, or a loaf of good bread—the warm power of the sun in Summer invites you to create, to produce, to make it happen.

HOT SUMMER PEACH-PLAY FOR LOVERS

This summer frolic is messy beyond belief, but it's also a wonderful way to celebrate the sensuality of summer with a loving partner.

Find the ripest, sweetest, juiciest peach you can. First, take turns holding it, sniffing it, stroking its fuzziness, touching it gently to your lips, to your cheek, then letting your tongues explore its skin. Gently break it open. Taste its juice.

Now, softly and slowly, caress each other with the open peach—break it in two, remove the pit, and then stroke its flesh all over each other. Gradually increase the pressure until you have globs of peach oozing delightfully everywhere. Then, savoring the experience, lick each other until all traces of peach are gone. (Well, *almost* all traces: this meditation will probably get pretty sticky.) If you are performing this exercise outdoors, be prepared for buggy visitors who will be irresistibly drawn to your warm stickiness. Making love covered with peach goop is a unique summer experience. And when it all gets to be a bit much, you can race each other for the shower or go jump in a lake—then afterglow turns into a refreshing tingle.

KITCHEN RITUALS FOR SUMMER SOLSTICE

The Summer Solstice is the longest day of the year. When it arrives (between June 20 and 23), you may want to spend some time honoring it. We have only this one chance to celebrate the glorious, vibrant circle of the sun at its strongest and most powerful.

Try simply noticing the light outside your kitchen window, becoming aware of sun-patterns on leaves and buildings, the colors of the shadows, the effortless way in which the sun can dry up a puddle or make a plant grow tall. Think about your own power to make things grow, to bring ideas and projects to fruition, to warm the people around you.

Choose golden, round things to eat today in honor of the sun, taking time to savor and appreciate the sunny shape and color and quality of the foods you fix. Something as simple as frying an egg or slicing an orange in rounds, if done with sun-consciousness, will make a satisfying connection with your inner Wild One and with the sun's vital power. If you feel like doing something more elaborate, you could make a round golden quiche (Juno's Summer Quiche, page 175, is ideal), or stoke up the grill and cook with real, living flame. Summer Solstice is the perfect time to celebrate fire. And you could decorate your stove and oven—representatives of fire in your kitchen—with some sunny flowers.

The Summer Solstice is a good day to put your hand-held cooking utensils outside to soak up some sunshine and sun-energy. Then, whenever you use them in the dark and chilly Winter to come, you will remember this simple, powerful act and be heartened.

Decorate your table with daisies, noticing how the flowers, with their rays of petals surrounding golden centers, mimic the round and fiery life-giver in the sky. Breathe your wishes for the harvest to come into the flowers, and know that your own precious life-energy will help to create whatever you want and need.

TITANIA'S CHERRY SOUP

serves 6

This midsummer night's dream of a first course would be right at home in a faerie court, sipped under the trees from tiny acorn cups. Its ambrosial flavor and delicate pink color make it a favorite with children, too. Titania's Cherry Soup reminds us of the summer orchards that rain delicious fruits down upon our heads with such amazing generosity.

> **2¹/₂ pounds fresh, dark sweet cherries**
> **4 cups water**
> **¹/₄ cup (or more to taste) honey, brown rice syrup, or maple syrup**
> **Juice of one lemon**
> **Whipped cream or yogurt as topping (optional)**

Wash and pit the cherries and place in a saucepan with the water and honey or maple syrup. Bring to a boil, then reduce heat and simmer for 15 to 20 minutes.

Remove 24 cherries and reserve.

Blend remaining cherries and liquid with lemon juice, and additional honey or syrup if needed (taste and see), until smooth.

Chill thoroughly.

To serve, ladle the soup into your prettiest bowls and top with the reserved cherries and a dollop of yogurt or whipped cream, if desired.

MIDSUMMER SALAD

serves 4 to 6

A round salad bowl filled with crisp, juicy, brightly colored vegetables makes a sunny centerpiece for your midsummer table.

Part of the fun of preparing this dish is using only what you like, only the freshest vegetables available. Taste the pleasures of exploration as you open a dark red beet—there are circles inside! Relish the vivid stripes of sliced red cabbage, or the blazing colors of peppers—experiment with yellow, orange, and purple ones, or fresh chilies with their varying shades of pale yellow-green.

Midsummer Salad is all about making tasty, vivid choices. Enjoy the many variations you can create to please yourself and your loved ones. The spicy heat and colorful beauty of the results will echo the summer world outside your doors.

Colorful selection of vegetables—choose from:
    Hot-colored bell peppers, julienned—try yellow, orange, red
    Beets, cut into thin circles or small cubes
    Red onion, thinly sliced or chopped
    Red cabbage, chopped
    Fresh jalapeno peppers or other hot peppers, thinly sliced or chopped
    Tomatoes, quartered, sliced, or chopped (experiment with unusual varieties—yellow or orange tomatoes add interest and excitement to your bowl)
    Red radishes, sliced
    Carrots, thinly sliced or julienned
    Fresh basil, parsley, or cilantro, chopped
Juice of half a lemon (optional)

In a large salad bowl, combine any or all of the vegetables.

Toss the salad with the juice of half a lemon, or with your favorite dressing, and serve.

SMOKY SUMMER VEGETABLES ON THE GRILL
(OR UNDER THE BROILER)

There is something truly magical about grilling. Our ancestors knew the mystery of sitting all together around flames that turned to glowing coals that—miraculously—transformed raw foods and gave them a special, smoky flavor touched by fire. Deep inside ourselves, we remember.

This simple recipe uses the power of fire in a way that our ancestors would have understood and enjoyed. The grill (or firepit or broiler) becomes a small emblem of the transformative sun that is making its power felt in so many positive ways at this time of year. Vegetables off the grill have a mouth-watering pungency that makes them both unusual and delicious. Don't be surprised if your vegetable-hating youngsters ask for seconds.

Part of the pleasure of this recipe lies in choosing the perfect vegetables to honor in the flames: when we really linger over the textures, colors, and shapes of eggplant, squash, or peppers, we allow our senses to be entranced.

Suggested vegetables:
  Whole ears of corn, husked and cleaned
  Green or red bell peppers, cut lengthwise into 1-inch wide strips
  Zucchini or yellow summer squash, cut lengthwise in quarters
  Red or white onions, cut into wedges
  Portabella or other mushrooms, thickly sliced
  Small to medium-sized eggplants, cut in 1/2-inch rounds
Good-quality olive oil or a Midsummer Marinade (below)

Take any or all of the suggested vegetables and brush or drizzle with good-quality olive oil (or marinate in any of the Midsummer Marinades provided below) and then place evenly on a hot grill, or underneath a hot broiler. Turn vegetables as necessary and keep an eye on them—when they are flecked with char and crisp-tender, they're done. Remove the vegetables to a serving platter as they reach the perfect doneness. Eggplant and onion usually take the longest to cook.

MIDSUMMER MARINADES

The basic ingredient for these recipes is olive oil, with varied additions to produce different flavorful delights.

In every case, whisk the ingredients together and allow vegetables to soak in the resulting marinade for at least 30 minutes before grilling.

HOT MAMA MARINADE

¹/₃ cup tamari or shoyu

¹/₄ cup good-quality olive oil

1 teaspoon dried mustard

¹/₂ to 1 teaspoon cayenne pepper (or more, depending on how hot you like it)

1 tablespoon Tabasco sauce (optional)

2 or 3 garlic cloves, crushed

SWEET AND TANGY MARINADE

¹/₃ cup tamari or shoyu

¹/₄ cup good-quality olive oil

¹/₄ cup maple syrup or honey

Juice of one lemon

Herbed Red Wine Marinade

¹/₂ cup full-bodied red wine

¹/₄ cup good-quality olive oil

2 garlic cloves, crushed

1 teaspoon salt

¹/₂ teaspoon each of any or all of the following dried herbs* (or 1 full teaspoon each if you use chopped fresh ones):

Marjoram	**Basil**
Thyme	**Sage**
Oregano	

THINGS TO DO WITH GRILLED VEGETABLES

Leftover grilled vegetables can become the basis of many nourishing and delicious summer meals, with minimal effort on your part.

- Try them plain on wholegrain bread. Stuff a baguette with them. Add a slice of provolone or some grated mozzarella—or Gruyère—and melt under the broiler. Or make special garlic bread by adding the grilled veggies, chopped fine, to the crushed garlic cloves.
- Make a rich and flavorful pasta sauce by simply mixing them with your favorite cooked pasta. You could also add a tomato, peeled and chopped, and a crushed garlic clove.

*Or you could place whole sprigs of fresh herbs—rosemary, marjoram, oregano, or thyme—on the vegetables as they grill.

- Add to pasta salads or your regular tossed garden salads.
- Chop fine, add a can of garbanzo beans, drained and mashed, and a crushed garlic clove. Use as a dip for pita or flatbread. Or add salsa and scoop it up with a taco chip. Chopped grilled vegetables are also delicious wrapped in large basil leaves.
- Grilled vegetables go well with rice, pilafs, couscous, and bulghur.
- Make your own mouth-watering burritos by filling flour tortillas with grilled vegetables, mashed cooked beans, salsa, and cheese.
- Add to your favorite gazpacho recipe. Or simply whiz the vegetables in a blender, thinning to the desired consistency with lemon juice and vegetable broth for a delicious chilled soup. Top with a dollop of sour cream, if desired.

FIERY RED BEANS AND RICE

serves 6

At the hottest time of the year, our thoughts inevitably turn to cultures that thrive on heat, and whose cuisines reflect a passion for spice. Rice and beans are a staple food for many people. This version—rich with tender vegetables and redolent with flavor—uses chipotle pepper to give it a special smoky taste. Fiery Red Beans and Rice becomes a delicious celebration of summer heat. Make it in honor of Akewa, the Argentine sun goddess who tells us that we are her sisters—only we are stranded here on Earth while she remains in the sky.

    2 to 3 tablespoons olive oil
    1 medium onion, chopped
    2 to 3 garlic cloves, crushed
    1 medium green bell pepper, seeded and chopped

1 medium dried chipotle pepper, coarsely chopped
1 teaspoon dried oregano
$^1/_2$ teaspoon cumin
$^1/_2$ teaspoon sea salt
$^1/_2$ teaspoon cayenne pepper (more or less, according to taste)
1 cup long-grain rice
2$^1/_2$ cups vegetable broth or water
1 15-ounce can small red beans, drained
3 tablespoons chopped fresh parsley

In a large saucepan, heat the olive oil over medium-high heat until fragrant. Then add the onion, garlic, green pepper, chipotle pepper, oregano, cumin, and sea salt and cayenne pepper to taste. Cook the vegetables, stirring often, about 10 to 15 minutes, until very tender.

Add the rice, stirring to coat with oil. Then add the vegetable broth or water and red beans and bring to a boil. Cover and simmer for 25 minutes, until rice is tender. Stir in parsley and serve.

ENCHANTED BERRIES

serves 4 to 6

This dish is sheer elfin enchantment when served after dark on a midsummer's night: the flickering of its mysterious violet-blue flames reminds us of magical winged creatures glimmering in the shadows just beyond our reach.

If you have either wild black or red raspberries in your own backyard or a mulberry tree that wants to share its sweet, subtle fruit, enlist the aid of friends and loved ones and pick a basketful: berries we've picked ourselves taste better than any other kind. But Enchanted Berries is also a magical way to enjoy the abundance of fresh raspberries you can find at any market this time of year.

Keep in mind that the alcohol in this recipe burns off, so children can feast upon it without a qualm.

3 cups wild berries or fresh raspberries, at room temperature or even warmer

1 tablespoon brown sugar

¹/₄ cup good-quality brandy, cognac, or dark rum, at room temperature or warmer

Yogurt or whipped cream as topping (optional)

In a flameproof chafing dish or bowl, place the wild berries or fresh raspberries and sprinkle with brown sugar.

Pour alcohol over berries. Cover the dish or bowl for a moment, then uncover and light the berries carefully with a match.

Watch the magic flames breathlessly until they're gone, then serve the berries with a dollop of yogurt or whipped cream, if desired.

DANCE OF THE LATE SUMMER GODDESS

You're never too old for a cuddle with your Big Mama: take a break from your hectic schedule and let me carry you in my arms for awhile. Put your feet on mine and I'll show you how to do a lazy waltz. My green outdoor world has been busy these past few weeks, too. But now my energy is slowly going within, pushing its way past the fruit to form the seeds that will grow next year. All of nature is breathing a sigh of contentment and relief—it's time to sit in the shade for a while. My fields are golden now, as golden as the grains that will keep your bellies warm in the cold months to come. Can you feel the days beginning to shorten? Let's make this a slow-dance to celebrate the joy I take in nourishing you. Because I do love to feed you, my grain dances willingly with the scythe so that you can have bread to eat.

August first is my favorite festival, a day for my children to honor the first harvest of the grains, and to celebrate the bread that is the "staff of life"—something you can lean on in times of need. It's a good day to be mindful of the food that keeps you alive.

Do you buy your bread wrapped in plastic from a supermarket shelf? Puffy, tasteless stuff filled with air and chemicals, mixed in great vats in factories far from the earth, the sun, the air—if you tried to lean on that, you'd fall—splat. My poor children—you are so rich in some ways, with foods on your tables that your ancestors could have never imagined—but so deprived in others.

Once, every loaf was sacred, the body of holy Mother Earth. Bread was thick and chewy then, rich with the earthiness of my grains, alive with taste and nourishment. But real bread is still within your reach. Even if it's only once a year, you can dance with a loaf or two and feel what it's like to enjoy the sensual pleasure of kneading and stroking that yummy, fleshlike dough.

Real home-baked bread will fill your kitchen with angels of blissmaking aroma that fly on brown, earthy wings. Real bread is nourishment for senses and spirit. As you mix it and knead *it and shape it, think of it as my body. And as you take your first bite, know that I am filling you with my loving energy.*

KITCHEN RITUALS FOR FIRST HARVEST

For many Western Europeans, August 1 was a traditional holy day in honor of the first grain harvest. Once called *Lammas*, literally "loaf-mass," it is the quintessential festival day for this book, since it celebrates the sacredness of food, the body of Mother Earth, in the form of bread.

Most of us simply don't have the time to bake regularly the way our great-grandmothers and great-great-grandmothers did. But if you do just a little planning in advance, most of us can usually carve out the time to bake bread once a year, beginning today. By slowing down and savoring each step of the process, we rediscover the blessings of bread with our hands, our hearts, and our starved spirits.

When your loaves are done, you may want to bless them by singing a song over them, or saying a prayer, or wafting a smudge stick or incense wand over them—or by simply touching them with your hands. Now tear off a piece of your bread and place it in your mouth. Close your eyes as you taste it. It is amazing how differently we feel about food when we cook it with the conscious intention of honoring its sacredness.

You can save a tiny bit of your special, sacred bread to place at your kitchen goddess's feet. Or wrap a piece in cloth and tuck it away until next year, when you can burn it outdoors or compost it, giving it back to the earth with thanks before you taste the first piece of your new bread. When we actively participate in simple, cyclical rituals like this one, year after year, we feel a sense of connection that goes a long way toward healing our spirit-wounds.

You may also want to make or buy a small wheat figure (or "corn dolly") today.

These harvest blessings were traditional in many cultures to honor the spirit of the wheat and bring luck and protection to the home. Craft shops sell lovely sheaves of wheat or barley which are easy to soak and braid. Tie with a green ribbon and hang over your oven. Or gather some dried grasses and do the same.

REAL EARTH-MOTHER WHOLE GRAIN BREAD

makes 2 loaves

Don't be daunted by the thought of making your own bread. It's really not difficult, and the time it takes is filled with pleasures, not just a chore to be suffered through. You actually spend more time waiting than anything else: waiting for the yeast to bubble, waiting for the stuff to cool, waiting for the dough to rise, waiting for it to rise again. This gives you lots of time to relax and dream. In fact, bread-baking is great for reducing stress. And the fragrance of baking bread is definitely aromatherapeutic.

$^1/_2$ **cup warm water**

2 tablespoons active dry yeast

1$^1/_2$ cups milk

2 cups rolled oats

3 tablespoons honey

2 tablespoons vegetable oil

1 teaspoon salt

$^1/_2$ **cup sesame seeds (optional)**

4 cups whole wheat flour

First, you have to wake up your yeast. In a small bowl, place the warm water (105°F–115°F) and sprinkle the yeast over it. Let this stand in a warm spot until the yeast bubbles, about 5 minutes.

Scald the milk, then put it in a large mixing bowl and stir in the rolled oats. Add the honey, vegetable oil, salt, and sesame seeds if desired.

Cool mixture to lukewarm and add 2 cups of the whole wheat flour. Beat well with a wooden spoon. Then add the yeast mixture and beat some more.

Add the remaining 2 cups whole wheat flour to make a soft dough. Turn out onto a floured surface and knead gently until smooth and elastic, about 10 minutes. (This is the really fun part. Good dough is a sensual experience to knead—warm, yielding, fleshy. *Mmmm!*)

Place the dough in a lightly oiled bowl, turning it so that all surfaces are oiled. Cover with a clean dishtowel, and let it rise in a warm place until doubled in size, about 1 hour.

Punch the dough down. Divide it in half and let it rest 10 minutes. Shape into 2 round loaves and place on a lightly greased baking sheet. Cover and let rise until doubled, about 40 minutes.

Toward the end of that 40 minutes, preheat oven to 350°F. Bake your loaves for 30 to 35 minutes, until golden brown. (Just wait until your home fills with bread-baking fragrance—Earthly paradise!) When the bread is done, the bottom crust will sound hollow when tapped. Take your loaves off the baking sheet immediately and let them cool on a rack.

You did it! Enjoy.

SHUCK BREAD

makes about 10 breads, shaped like small ears of corn

This recipe is a lot of fun to make, looks charming when done, and is deliciously satisfying. It makes a good alternative for people with sensitivities to wheat, or for those of you who prefer to honor the traditional bread festival spending a few hours relaxing outdoors by a campfire rather than making bread in the kitchen. (In fact, this is a variation of a Girl Scout recipe given to me by Jessica Kemper, dear sister and super-woman, who has made this bread on camping trips with the troop.) And Shuck Bread teaches us to use every bit of the corn, shucks as well as kernels. (After you've finished scraping the cobs, you could carve them into little goddesses and leave them to dry in the sun. Then you can place one on your kitchen windowsill as a perpetual reminder of this warm and glorious festival day.)

1 cup fine-ground yellow corn meal

$1/3$ cup fresh corn, scraped right off the cob (reserve the husks leftover from shucking the corn)

1 egg

2 tablespoons melted butter or mild-tasting olive oil

1 teaspoon baking powder

$1/2$ teaspoon salt

Water (enough to form a thick dough)

$3/4$ cup shredded cheese (optional)

$1/4$ cup chopped jalapeno peppers (optional)

Oil for coating husks

Salt and butter as seasoning (optional)

In a large bowl, combine the cornmeal, corn, egg, olive oil or melted butter, baking powder, salt, and water (as needed)—along with the shredded cheese and jalapeno peppers if desired—until mixture forms a thick dough.

Choose 2 or 3 thicknesses of husks from your fresh corn for each shuck bread. Stack the husks together, insides facing up, and lightly brush the top husk with oil. Place 2 to 3 tablespoonfuls of dough mixture in the center of this bed of husks.

Fold the husk edges so that dough is completely encased in a long corn-shaped packet. Tie each end shut, using a long strip of husk or string.

Wrap each bread with aluminum foil and place the little packages in the coals of a campfire or grill.*

Bake until bread resists light finger pressure (it will stop feeling pasty). Untie one end and fold husks down—it will look charmingly like an ear of corn. Sprinkle with salt and butter, if you like, and eat.

* If you don't have a campfire handy, you may boil or steam these, or panfry them in a little vegetable oil, or bake them at 400°F. In all cases, cook until the breads resist light finger pressure.

LATE SUMMER RECIPES

TOMATO VENUS SOUP

serves 4 to 6

Did you know that tomatoes were once known as "love apples" and are sacred to Venus? And did you know that Venus is not only the ancient Roman goddess of love—she's also the goddess of kitchen gardens? This Venusian treat is one of my favorite summer soups—effortless to make, but with a surprisingly complex taste that evokes warm days and sun-drenched earth. Its vivid color and mouth-watering flavor are sure to please. Make a potful tonight for the ones you love.

1 quart canned crushed tomatoes

3 or 4 large ripe tomatoes, chopped

$\frac{1}{4}$ cup oil-packed sundried tomatoes, drained and chopped

$\frac{1}{4}$ cup finely chopped red onion

1 garlic clove, crushed

2 tablespoons chopped fresh basil, or 1 tablespoon dried

2 tablespoons olive oil

2 tablespoons freshly squeezed lemon juice

Sea salt (or tamari) to taste

Freshly ground black pepper to taste

1 or 2 tablespoons melted butter (optional)

Sour cream as topping (optional)

4 to 6 fresh basil leaves for garnish (optional)

In a bowl if serving chilled, or in a saucepan if you plan to serve warm, combine the crushed tomatoes, chopped tomatoes, and sundried tomatoes, red onion, garlic, basil, olive oil, lemon juice, and sea salt (or tamari) and black pepper to taste.

If you're serving this soup warm you may want to add 1 or 2 tablespoons melted butter. Warm or cold, it's delicious with a dollop of sour cream and/or a small fresh basil leaf for each serving.

CRUNCHY SUMMER SALADS

Late Summer is seed time, when the Earth Mother sends her energies into those little packages of power that will rest in Winter's earth and then waken to make new life in Spring. We can enjoy the tasty nutrients that are so concentrated in seeds—and make our tossed salads late-Summer special—by adding any of the following to our garden greens:

Pumpkin seeds, either raw or toasted in the oven with tamari and cayenne

Shelled sunflower seeds

Sesame seeds

Poppy seeds

Dock seeds from your backyard—they add crunch and a pleasing reddish brown color

You could even try adding a few seeds from your bell peppers, rather than tossing them in the compost!

SIMPLE-GIFTS MILLET

serves 4 to 6

Millet, which many of us used to think was for the birds, is now being rediscovered as a delicious and economical source of excellent nutrition—certainly not just so much birdseed.

Millet is one of nature's simplest but most delightful gifts; it is the perfect summer offering because its adorably round and golden grains are so reminiscent of the summer sun. Its delicate, nutlike taste makes a perfect foil for Mama Zabetta's Spicy Stir-fried Greens.

1 cup millet
2 cups water (or vegetable broth)
¹/₂ teaspoon sea salt (or less, to taste)
1 garlic clove, crushed (optional)
1 tablespoon butter (optional)
Toasted sesame seeds (optional)

Rinse the millet in warm water several times to remove any bitterness, then drain. Place in a saucepan with the water and add sea salt to taste.

Bring to a boil, cover, reduce heat to low, and simmer for 30 to 40 minutes, until water is completely absorbed.

Variations on this recipe include adding a crushed garlic clove to the cooking millet, or a tablespoon of butter, or some toasted sesame seeds. Or you could cook your millet in vegetable broth rather than water.

Serve cooked millet plain, with butter if desired, or topped with the Spicy Stir-fried Greens (below). Leftover cooked millet may be tossed with chopped vegetables and a simple salad dressing for a quick and delicious cold salad.

MAMA ZABETTA'S SPICY STIR-FRIED GREENS

serves 4 to 6

Mama Zabetta (a.k.a. Elizabeth Cunningham—novelist, dear friend, and fellow food-lover) cooked this up for us one steamy late Summer evening and the resulting feast became a true celebration of the season, enjoyed with gusto by all. Redolent with tastes and textures, this spicy dish reminds us of both heat and bounty—two of Summer's favorite watchwords.

Half the fun of preparing this luscious dish is adding things with a playful, liberal hand. As Zabetta forcefully reminds us, "Less isn't more. MORE is more!" Cast the crushed red pepper flakes about the pan with goddesslike generosity.

Be sure to keep adding olive oil whenever needed—the result should be moist, never dry. Greens should predominate in this dish, but the choice of ingredients and their amounts are strictly up to you. Embrace your goddess power!

2 to 3 tablespoons olive oil

Onions, chopped

Garlic cloves, chopped

Dried mustard

Chopped chilies or crushed red pepper flakes

Assorted slower-cooking vegetables (as desired):

    Beets

    Bell peppers

    Zucchini or summer squash

    Cauliflower

    Broccoli

Tamari or shoyu

Dry red wine (optional)

Assorted faster-cooking vegetables (as desired):

    Swiss chard

Beet greens
Chinese cabbage
Toasted sesame seeds or sunflower seeds
Cashew, pecan, or almond pieces
Toasted sesame oil
Fresh parsley, chopped

Heat olive oil in a large saucepan or wok over medium-high heat until fragrant. Add the onions, garlic, dried mustard, and chilies or pepper flakes. Stir occasionally until vegetables are golden and tender.

Meanwhile, chop any or all of the slower-cooking vegetables and add, along with a sprinkle of tamari or shoyu and dry red wine if desired.

Add olive oil as needed to keep ingredients shiny and moist and stir occasionally, preferably while swigging an icy-cold beer. Add some more red pepper flakes. And maybe a little more tamari.

When everything is just crisp-tender, chop any or all of the faster-cooking vegetables and add, continuing to cook for just a couple of minutes, until the greens are barely wilted.

Add a handful or so of toasted sesame seeds or sunflower seeds and either cashew, pecan, or almond pieces.

Drizzle with toasted sesame oil and toss. Serve topped with chopped fresh parsley over a bed of your favorite cooked grain—brown rice, bulghur, couscous, quinoa, or Simple-Gifts Millet.

SUNNY PEACH PIE

The amber glory of this sun-shaped dessert, as well as its mouth-watering aroma and flavor, satisfies us deeply in many ways. When we create a little sun that feeds us so deliciously, our hearts are warmed by this embodiment of the sun's power. Celebrate that power in yourself. And, if you are so inclined, you could try making your sun-connection even stronger by baking this pie in the early morning as you watch the sun come up. As you arrange your peach slices in their circular pattern, think of the Scandinavian goddess Sunna, who sits and spins with her golden distaff so that the sun will rise.

1 unbaked pie crust (try Wholemeal Crust, Classic No-Dairy Crust, or Graham Cracker Crust—recipe follows)

3 to 4 cups sliced fresh peaches

2 teaspoons unbleached flour

$1/4$ cup peach preserves (the kind with no added sugar)

1 teaspoon freshly squeezed lemon juice

$1/2$ teaspoon ground cinnamon

Freshly grated nutmeg

Dash of sea salt

Preheat oven to 400°F.

In the unbaked crust of your choice, place the peach slices, arranged in overlapping concentric circles. Sprinkle peaches with flour.

Combine the peach preserves, lemon juice, cinnamon, nutmeg, and dash of sea salt in a saucepan and heat until hot.

Pour this glaze over the peaches and bake in preheated oven for 10 minutes, then turn the heat down to 375°F and continue baking for an additional 30 to 35 minutes. May be served warm, at room temperature, or cold.

GRAHAM CRACKER CRUST

enough for one 9-inch pie bottom

This simple recipe makes a tasty base for baked fruit pies.

¾ cup crushed Graham crackers
¼ cup melted butter

In a medium bowl, thoroughly combine the crushed Graham crackers and melted butter.
   Press firmly into the bottom of a a 9-inch pie plate.
   Fill and bake as directed in recipe.

LAST WORD OF THE SUMMER GODDESS

The beauty of my last slow dance always inspires my sister Autumn. Now you will have her songs to keep you company as you begin the descent into darkness and cold. It will be many months before I take your hands and swing you into my dance again. It is hard to let you go.

Now we dance a dance of stillness for just a moment, a moment of timeless pause. Your stillness honors me. As my daughter Diane Mariechild reminds you, "We are too busy doing. We are human beings. Today, remember to be."

WILD WOMAN TIPS
FOR ACTING OUT IN
THE KITCHEN

The kitchen is the perfect place to honor our feelings. Many of us spend a lot of time there, often alone. We have a Power Place in the kitchen; it feels like safe space. What better spot to act out our aggressions and frustrations (as well as our more positive emotions) than in the kitchen?

Action and intention can be powerful allies when we cook. When we give our inner Wild Woman a conscious activity to perform, one that is rooted in what we are feeling right now, we place our feet on the path toward greater self-acceptance. Most of us are busy trying to heal ourselves from the deadly effects of our culture; our time in the kitchen can be used wisely and well to nurture that process along.

Here are a few ideas to help you get started. You will doubtlessly find your own ways to practice self-healing in the kitchen.

For those emotional, weepy days: Chop a lot of onions. Let the tears flow. Make exaggerated crying noises.

For excess anger and aggression: Try the karate method of peeling garlic cloves.

Place the clove on a chop board. With a hefty kitchen knife in your hand, focus your anger on the clove (it won't mind), take a deep breath, place the handle flat on the garlic, and whap it hard with your fist, yelling *Hi-yah*, if desired. For serious anger, buy plates for a nickel at the thrift shop and throw them in the sink. The sound of breaking crockery is very releasing.

When you're in the process of shedding old, outgrown stuff in your life: Peel some root vegetables with a peeler (this is a good idea if your produce is not organic). As the curls of skin come peeling off, enjoy the freshness of the surface underneath. Imagine your own life beginning fresh and new.

To get your energies going: Shake up a batch of salad dressing in a jar. Get your whole body into the act. Be rhythmic. Let your jar of dressing become your maracas. Sing a Latino song. Shake those hips.

When you're feeling peaceful and calm (or to get yourself that way): Cook something that takes a lot of slow stirring (like Risotto Primavera, for instance). Let yourself drift and dream as you stir. Stirring can help us feel more sensuous, too.

When you feel confused or spacey: After you chop something into a pile, push it around on your chop board and make patterns with it. Order your ingredients according to color. Clean out a drawer or cupboard.

When you're afraid: Sit on the countertop with your feet in the sink and run warm water on them. Hold something in your hand that grew in the ground—a potato, a beet, a turnip. Remind yourself that you are a child of the Earth Mother.

When you need to synthesize or get something together: Blending is great for this. It is pure magic to see how several very disparate things will homogenize beautifully after just a few seconds in the blender. Use a pureed soup recipe—Goddess's Green Pea or Sensuous Spinach, for instance.

When you want to feel more in touch with nature: Try a wild foods recipe, like Wild Salad, White Pine Tea, or Daylily-Bud Sauté. Going outside and gathering the ingredients is guaranteed to lift your spirits and make you feel more connected to the Earth Mother.

When you can't stand the thought of cooking: Take a trip to a farmer's market or natural foods store. Look for ingredients so fresh that they practically vibrate with energy or for other more unusual things that might interest you.

Reading fiction is another way to get motivated in the kitchen. Years ago, a book-loving friend confided, "I always crave the foods I'm reading about. Peter Mayle's books on Provence made me hungry for eggplants and garlic. I drink a lot of tea and munch scones when I read Agatha Christie. And when I was reading *Clan of the Cave Bear*, I kept wanting to forage outside for stuff." (Unfortunately, she lived in lower Manhattan at the time.)

Another friend was inspired to take a class in Chinese cooking after she read *The Kitchen God's Wife*, by Amy Tan; another went on a Mexican food kick while reading Laura Esquivel's *Like Water for Chocolate*. Colette's books always make me want café au lait and crusty French bread. Visit a library; see what whets *your* appetite.

Try listening to appropriate music while you cook. I sometimes like to play Italian opera when I'm making pasta, for instance—it helps to get me in the mood. Cajun food and Cajun music are a natural match. Edith Piaf is great for French food. Experiment.

Cooking in sync with your monthly cycle: Many of us find that our feelings about food change with our hormonal tides. I feel more like cooking when I'm pre-menstrual than at any other time in my cycle—so I cook extra on those days and freeze some to save for ovulation when I'd rather be doing other things instead. On the days when I feel especially mentally alert, I make up menus and shopping lists. If I'm in a sociable phase, I have friends over for potlucks or community cooks. When I'm feeling more hermit-like (especially in Winter), I do lots of baking and take that quiet time to write or dream. When we pay attention to our moods and honor them in the kitchen, we honor our goddess-selves. Honor what you're feeling today.

SUGGESTED READING

The following lists are good jumping-off places for your own explorations into green housekeeping, the Goddess, earth-centered spirituality, herbs, aromatherapy, rituals, and other delights. Many of these selections include detailed bibliographies that will lead you deeper: trust your own ability to find what you need.

AROMATHERAPY

Berwick, Ann. *Holistic Aromatherapy: Balance the Body and Soul with Essential Oils*. St. Paul, MN: Llewellyn, 1994.

Cunningham, Scott. *The Complete Book of Incense, Oils and Brews*. St. Paul, MN: Llewellyn, 1992.

Davis, Patricia. *Aromatherapy A–Z*. Great Britain: C. W. Daniel, 1988.

Dye, Jane. *Aromatherapy for Women and Children*. Great Britain: C. W. Daniel, 1992.

Tisserand, Maggie. *Aromatherapy for Women*. Rochester, VT: Inner Traditions, 1988.

COOKBOOKS, BOOKS ABOUT COOKING AND FOOD

Alper, Nicole, and Lynette Rohrer. *Wild Women in the Kitchen: 101 Rambunctious Recipes & 99 Tasty Tales*. Berkeley, CA: Conari Press, 1996.

Callan, Ginny. *Horn of the Moon Cookbook*. New York: Harper and Row, 1987.

————. *Beyond the Moon Cookbook*. New York: HarperCollins, 1996.

Colwin, Laurie. *Home Cooking: A Writer in the Kitchen*. New York: HarperCollins, 1988.

d'Avila-Latourrette, Brother Victor-Antoine. *This Good Food: Contemporary French Vegetarian Recipes from a Monastery Kitchen*. Woodstock, NY: Overlook Press, 1993.

Hurd, Frank J., and Rosalie Hurd. *Ten Talents Cookbook*. Collegedale, TN: The College Press, 1968.

Katzen, Mollie. *The Enchanted Broccoli Forest*. Berkeley, CA: Ten Speed Press, 1982.

————. *Moosewood Cookbook*. Berkeley, CA: Ten Speed Press, 1977.

————. *Still Life with Menu Cookbook*. Berkeley, CA: Ten Speed Press, 1994.

Kavasch, Barrie. *Native Harvests: Recipes and Botanicals of the American Indian*. New York: Vintage Books, 1979.

Lair, Cynthia. *Feeding the Whole Family: Down-to-Earth Cookbook and Whole Foods Guide*. San Diego: LuraMedia, 1994.

Nearing, Helen. *Simple Food for the Good Life*. Walepole, NH: Stillpoint Publishing, 1985.

Robertson, Laurel, Carol Flinders, and Brian Ruppenthal. *Laurel's Kitchen Recipes*. Berkeley, CA: Ten Speed Press, 1993.

————. *The New Laurel's Kitchen: A Handbook for Vegetarian Cookery & Nutrition*. Berkeley, CA: Ten Speed Press, 1976.

Rombauer, Irma, and Marion Rombauer Becker. *Joy of Cooking*. New York: Penguin, 1973.

Shaw, Maura D., and Sydna Altschuler Byrne. *Foods from Mother Earth: A Basic Cookbook for Young Vegetarians (and Anybody Else)*. Wappingers Falls, NY: Shawangunk Press, 1994.

Thomas, Anna. *The Vegetarian Epicure*. New York: Random House, 1972.

————. *The Vegetarian Epicure, Book Two*. New York: Alfred A. Knopf, 1978.

————. *The New Vegetarian Epicure*. New York: Alfred A. Knopf, 1996.

Vitell, Bettina. *A Taste of Heaven and Earth*. New York: HarperCollins, 1993.

Waters, Alice. *Chez Panisse Vegetables*. New York: HarperCollins, 1996.

———. *Fanny at Chez Panisse*. New York: HarperCollins, 1992.

EARTH-CENTERED SPIRITUALITY, THE GODDESS, RITUAL

Beck, Renee, and Sydney Barbara Metrick. *The Art of Ritual*. Berkeley, CA: Celestial Arts, 1990.

Blair, Nancy. *Amulets of the Goddess*. Oakland, CA: Wingbow Press, 1993.

Bolen, Jean Shinoda. *Goddesses in Everywoman: A New Psychology of Women*. New York: Harper and Row, 1984.

Budapest, Z. *Grandmother Moon: Lunar Magic in Our Lives*. San Francisco: HarperSanFrancisco, 1991.

———. *The Goddess in the Office*. San Francisco: HarperSanFrancisco, 1993.

———. *The Grandmother of Time*. San Francisco: HarperSanFrancisco, 1989.

———. *The Holy Book of Women's Mysteries*. Vols. 1 and 2. Berkeley, CA: Wingbow Press, 1986 rev.

Cahill, Sedonia, and Joshua Halpern. *Ceremonial Circle: Practice, Ritual, and Renewal for Personal and Community Healing*. San Francisco: HarperSanFrancisco, 1992.

Campanelli, Pauline. *Ancient Ways: Reclaiming Pagan Traditions*. St. Paul, MN: Llewellyn, 1991.

———. *Wheel of the Year: Living the Magickal Life*. St. Paul, MN: Llewellyn, 1987.

Carr-Gomm, Philip, and Stephanie Carr-Gomm. *The Druid Animal Oracle: Working with the Sacred Animals of Druid Tradition*. New York: Simon and Schuster, 1994.

Duerk, Judith. *Circle of Stones*. San Diego: LuraMedia, 1989.

Edwards, Carolyn McVickar. *The Storyteller's Goddess: Tales of the Goddess and Her Wisdom from around the World*. New York: HarperCollins, 1991.

Eisler, Riane. *The Chalice and the Blade: Our History, Our Future.* San Francisco: HarperSanFrancisco, 1986.

Gimbutas, Marija. *The Language of the Goddess.* San Francisco: HarperSanFrancisco, 1989.

Johnson, Cait, and Maura D. Shaw. *Celebrating the Great Mother: A Handbook of Earth-Honoring Activities for Parents and Children.* Rochester, VT: Destiny Books, 1995.

Monaghan, Patricia. *The Book of Goddesses and Heroines.* New York: E. P. Dutton, 1981.

Mutén, Burleigh, ed. *Return of the Great Goddess.* Boston: Shambhala, 1994.

Nahmad, Claire. *Earth Magic: A Wisewoman's Guide to Herbal, Astrological, and Other Folk Wisdom.* Rochester, VT: Destiny Books, 1994.

Noble, Vicki. *Motherpeace: A Way to the Goddess through Myth, Art and Tarot.* San Francisco: Harper and Row, 1983.

———. *Shakti Woman: Feeling Our Fire, Healing Our World.* San Francisco: HarperSanFrancisco, 1991.

Sjöö, Monica, and Barbara Mor. *The Great Cosmic Mother: Rediscovering the Religion of the Earth.* San Francisco: HarperSanFrancisco, 1987.

Starhawk. *The Spiral Dance: A Rebirth of the Ancient Religion of the Great Goddess: Rituals, Invocations, Exercises, Magic.* San Francisco: Harper and Row, 1989.

Starck, Marcia. *Women's Medicine Ways: Cross-Cultural Rites of Passage.* Freedom, CA: Crossing Press, 1993.

Stein, Diane. *The Women's Spirituality Book.* St. Paul, MN: Llewellyn, 1987.

Stone, Merlin. *Ancient Mirrors of Womanhood: Our Goddess and Heroine Heritage.* New York: New Sibylline, 1979.

———. *When God Was a Woman.* New York: Harcourt Brace Jovanovich, 1978.

Swain, Sally. *Oh My Goddess!* New York: Penguin, 1994.

Teish, Luisa. *Jambalaya: The Natural Woman's Book of Personal Charms and Practical Rituals.* San Francisco: Harper and Row, 1985.

Waldherr, Kris. *The Book of Goddesses.* Hillsboro, OR: Beyond Words Publishing, 1995.

Walker, Barbara G. *The Crone.* San Francisco: Harper and Row, 1985.

———. *The Woman's Dictionary of Symbols & Sacred Objects.* San Francisco: HarperSanFrancisco, 1988.

———. *The Woman's Encyclopedia of Myths and Secrets.* San Francisco: Harper and Row, 1983.

———. *Women's Rituals.* San Francisco: Harper and Row, 1990.

Weinstein, Marion. *Earth Magic: A Dianic Book of Shadows.* Custer, WA: Phoenix, 1986.

Wilshire, Donna. *Virgin Mother Crone: Myths and Mysteries of the Triple Goddess.* Rochester, VT: Inner Traditions, 1994.

Worth, Valerie. *The Crone's Book of Words.* St. Paul, MN: Llewellyn, 1986.

FOOD FOR THOUGHT

These are a few of my personal touchstones—books that, although they don't exactly fit into any of the other categories in this suggested list, have made a positive difference in my life. One common thread that connects these very different authors is a deep appreciation of women and of the Earth, and an awareness of the sacred in the everyday. While our culture conspires to put our spirits to sleep, these will wake you up. You may find, after sampling a few of these offerings, that you are inspired to begin a list of your own. Share it with your friends!

Ackerman, Diane. *A Natural History of the Senses.* New York: Random House, 1990.

Bender, Sue. *Everyday Sacred: A Woman's Journey Home.* New York: HarperCollins, 1995.

———. *Plain and Simple: A Woman's Journey to the Amish.* New York: Harper Collins, 1989.

Cameron, Julia. *The Artist's Way: A Spiritual Path to Higher Creativity.* NY: Putnam, 1992.

Colette. Any of her novels; even her biographies are delicious. This woman had a real passion for life and for good food.

Cunningham, Elizabeth. *The Return of the Goddess.* Barrytown, NY: Station Hill Press, 1992.

Estes, Clarissa Pinkola. *Women Who Run with the Wolves: Myths and Stories of the Wild Woman Archetype*. New York: Ballantine, 1992.

Fisher, M. F. K. Anything you can find of hers is valuable, but *The Art of Eating* is especially wonderful.

Linthwaite, Illona, ed. *Ain't I a Woman! A Book of Women's Poetry from Around the World*. New York: Random House, 1993.

Louden, Jennifer. *The Woman's Comfort Book: A Self-Nurturing Guide for Restoring Balance in Your Life*. San Francisco: HarperSanFrancisco, 1992.

Martz, Sandra, ed. *When I Am an Old Woman, I Shall Wear Purple*. Watsonville, CA: Papier-Mâché Press, 1987.

Perkins, John. *The World Is As You Dream It: Shamanic Teachings from the Amazon and Andes*. Rochester, VT: Inner Traditions, 1994.

Sarton, May. Any of the journals, but especially *Journal of a Solitude* and *Plant Dreaming Deep*.

Scott, Anne. *Serving Fire: Food for Thought, Body, and Soul*. Berkeley, CA: Celestial Arts, 1994.

Williams, Terry Tempest. *An Unspoken Hunger*. New York: Random House, 1994.

GREEN HOUSEKEEPING

Berthold-Bond, Annie. *Clean and Green: The Complete Guide to Nontoxic and Environmentally Safe Housekeeping*. Woodstock, NY: Ceres Press, 1990.

Berthold-Bond, Annie, and Mothers and Others. *The Green Kitchen Handbook*. New York: HarperCollins, 1997.

Dadd, Debra Lynn. *The Nontoxic Home: Protecting Yourself and Your Family from Everyday Toxics and Health Hazards*. Los Angeles: Jeremy P. Tarcher, 1986.

———. *Nontoxic, Natural, & Earthwise: How to Protect Yourself and Your Family from Harmful Products and Live in Harmony with the Earth*. Los Angeles: Jeremy P. Tarcher, 1990.

———. *Sustaining the Earth: Choosing Consumer Products That Are Safe for You, Your Family, and the Earth.* Los Angeles: Jeremy P. Tarcher, 1994.

HERBS, MAGICAL FOODS, WILD FOODS

Berneth, Stefen. *Common Weeds.* Mineola, NY: Dover, 1976.

Beyerl, Paul. *The Master Book of Herbalism.* Custer, WA: Phoenix, 1984.

Cunningham, Scott. *Cunningham's Encyclopedia of Magical Herbs.* St. Paul, MN: Llewellyn, 1985.

———. *Magical Herbalism.* St. Paul, MN: Llewellyn, 1983.

———. *The Magic in Food.* St. Paul, MN: Llewellyn, 1991.

Griggs, Barbara. *The Green Witch Herbal: Restoring Nature's Magic in Home, Health, and Beauty Care.* Rochester, VT: Inner Traditions, 1994.

Mabey, Richard, ed. *The New Age Herbal.* New York: Macmillan, 1988.

Shanberg, Karen, and Stan Tekiela. *Plantworks: Field Guide, Recipes, Activities.* Cambridge, MN: Adventure, 1991.

Weed, Susun. *Healing Wise.* Woodstock, NY: Ash Tree Publishing, 1989.

MEDITATION, MINDFULNESS, SPIRITUAL PRACTICE

Ban Breathnach, Sarah. Simple *Abundance: A Daybook of Comfort and Joy.* New York: Warner Books, 1995.

Cowan, Tom. *Shamanism as a Spiritual Practice for Daily Life.* Freedom, CA: Crossing Press, 1996.

Gawain, Shakti. *Creative Visualization.* Mill Valley, CA: Whatever Publishing, 1978.

Hanh, Thich Nhat. *The Miracle of Mindfulness: A Manual on Meditation.* Boston: Beacon Press, 1987.

Mariechild, Diane. *Mother Wit: A Guide to Healing and Psychic Development.* Freedom, CA: Crossing Press, 1988.

————. *Open Mind: Women's Daily Inspiration for Becoming Mindful.* San Francisco: HarperSanFrancisco, 1995.

Moore, Thomas. *Care of the Soul: A Guide for Cultivating Depth and Sacredness in Everyday Life.* NY: HarperCollins, 1992.

NATIVE AMERICAN ISSUES

Brave Bird, Mary, with Richard Erdoes. *Ohitika Woman.* New York: Grove Press, 1993.

Brown, Dee. *Bury My Heart at Wounded Knee.* New York: Holt, Rinehart, Winston, 1970.

Crow Dog, Mary. *Lakota Woman.* New York: HarperCollins, 1990.

Farley, Ronnie. *Women of the Native Struggle: Portraits and Testimony of Native American Women.* New York: Orion, 1993.

Matthiessen, Peter. *In the Spirit of Crazy Horse.* New York: Penguin, 1992.

PUBLICATIONS

A Real Life, 245 Eighth Ave., Box 400, New York, NY 10011.

The Beltane Papers: A Journal of Women's Mysteries, P.O. Box 29694, Bellingham, WA 98228-1694.

SageWoman: Celebrating the Goddess in Every Woman, P.O. Box 641, Point Arena, CA 95468-0641.

SUPPLIES

It isn't always possible to get what you need locally. If you can't find mugwort or god-dess statues anywhere nearby, try these mail-order suppliers: they offer inspiration as well as the things you need. Call or write for catalogs, some of which are beautiful enough to frame.

COOKING GADGETS

Gooseberry Patch
P.O. Box 190
Delaware, OH 43015
(800) 854-6673
(they have great cookie-cutters—
including leaf-shaped ones, and an
appreciation of the seasons)

Williams-Sonoma
P.O. Box 7456
San Francisco, CA 94120-7456
(800) 541-2233

EARTH-CONSCIOUS HOME PRODUCTS

(all-natural cleaning products, recycled papers, natural fabrics, and more)

Earth Care
Ukiah, CA 95842-8507
(800) 347-0070

Real Goods
555 Leslie Street
Ukiah, CA 95482-3471
(800) 762-7325

Seventh Generation
360 Interlocken Blvd., Suite 300
Broomfield, CO 80021
(800) 456-1177

GODDESS GOODIES

(books, statues, jewelry, meditation
tools, and much more)

Isabella
2780 Via Orange Way, Suite B
Spring Valley, CA 91978
(800) 777-5205
(books, jewelery, many lovely things)

Jane Iris Designs, Inc.
P.O. Box 608
Graton, CA 95444
(800) 828-5687
(jewelry)

JBL Statues
Images of the Divine
P.O. Box 163
Crozet, VA 22932
(800) 290-6203
jblstatue@jblstatue.com
http://www.jblstatue.com

(over 150 images of dieties and arche-
types from around the world: send $2
for catalog)

Kate Cartwright
Box 103
Graton, CA 95444
(rubber stamps: send $1 for catalog)
katecart@nbn.com
http://www.nbn.com/people/katecart

M'Lou Brubaker
30 Bohn Road
Goodland, MN 55742
(218) 492-4487
(jewelry)

Mountain Rose Herbs
20818 High Street
North San Juan, CA 95960
(800) 879-3337
(916) 292-9138
(catalog of herbal delights)

Pleiades
P.O. Box 389
Brimfield, MA 01010-0389
(413) 245-9484
(goddess figures, jewelry)

The Pyramid Collection
P.O. Box 3333, Altid Park
Chelmsford, MA 01824-0933
(800) 333-4220
(meditation tools, books, candles,
tapes, etc.)

Star River Productions
The Great Goddess Collection
P.O. Box 510642
Melbourne Beach, FL 32951
(800) 232-1733
(sacred art, sculpture, jewelry, and books
by Nancy Blair)

Woman of Wands
Route 102
P.O. Box 330
South Lee, MA 01260
(413) 243-4036
Fax: (413) 243-0569
wowbyn@vgernet.net
(goddess and Wiccan books,
Tarot decks, goddess statues
and plaques, more)

HERBS

Blessed Herbs
109 Barre Plains Road
Oakham, MA 01068
(800) 489-4372
(508) 882-3755
(organic and wildcrafted herbs
and liquid extracts)

Green Terrestrial
P.O. Box 266
Milton, NY 12547
(914) 795-5238

Mountain Rose Herbs
20818 High Street
North San Juan, CA 95960
(800) 879-3337
(916) 292-9138

INDEX

Akewa, 189

Almonds, toasted, 161

Angelica, 12

Aphrodite, 163

Aphrodite's Love Cakes, 163–64

Apples, 12

    Fig–Apple Crumble, 66

    pie, 77–78

    salad, 61, 73

    soup, 46

    Sweet Potato–Apple Bake, 75

Appliances, personalizing, 17–19

Apron making, 28–32

Asparagus, 160

Autumn, 40–45

Autumn Equinox, 54–56

    recipes for, 46–78

    Samhain, 43, 68–72, 73, 77

Autumn Cider Dressing, 74

Autumn Equinox, 54–56

Basil, 12

Baubo, 55

Beans

    and rice, 189–90

soup, 118–20

sprouted, 141

stew, 50

Beltane, 32, 156

Beltane Asparagus, 160

Berries, 177–78, 191

Bread

    baking, 193

    corn, 196–97

    soup, 59–60

    stuffing, 64–65

    whole-grain, 194–95

Brigid, 136–37, 139

Brigid's Broth of Inspiration, 139–41

Cailleach, 72

Cailleach (Kale–Leek) Soup, 72–73

Cake

    Aphrodite's Love Cakes, 163–64

    Simple Strawberry Shortcake, 177–78

    Waking Earth Cake, 144–45

Candy, maple, 153–54

Carrots, 122

Chairs for kitchen, selecting, 15–17

Chamomile, 12

Chard, 62

Cherries, soup, 184

Cinnamon, 12–13

Cleaning, kitchen, 10–15, 129

    natural products for, 11

Clove, 13

Composting, 11–12

Cooking

    as emotional release, 205–7

    family memories about, 6

    rituals for, 33–34

    as a sacred act, 1–3, 7–8

    supplies, resources for, 216–18

Corn

    bread, 196–97

    skillet cakes, 96

    stew, 50

    tarts, with greens and hazelnuts, 48–49

Cranberries, with green beans, 110

Creamy Cashew Sauce, 63

Daylily-Bud Sauté, 174

Demeter, 54–55, 66
Demeter's Soothing Oat-Bread
        Soup, 59–60
Eggs, 130–31, 147, 152
        omelet, mushroom, 152–53
        quiche, 175–76
Enchanted Berries, 191
Eucalyptus, 13
Evergreen, 13, 83, 84
Fennel, 13
Festive Green Beans with
        Cranberries, 110
Fiery Red Beans and Rice, 189–90
Fig–Apple Crumble, 66
Flowering Salad, 172–73
Food, erotic nature of, 32, 156
Fruit, dried, 124–25
Goddesses, 22–23, 27–28, 32,
        136–37, 139, 163, 175, 189,
        198, 203
Goddess's Green Pea Soup, 171–72
Green beans, with cranberries, 110
Heartha, 94
Heartha's Roasted Winter
        Vegetables, 94–95
Herb correspondences, 12–14
Holidays, Celtic. See also Meditations
        Autumn Equinox, 54–56
        Beltane, 32, 156
        Imbolc, 136–37
        Lammas, 193–94
        Samhain, 43, 68–72, 73, 77
        Spring Equinox, 146–48
        Summer Solstice, 182–83
        Winter Solstice, 84, 103–8
Imbolc, 136–37

Irish soda bread, 138
Juno, 175
Juno's Summer Quiche, 175–76
Kale
        skillet cakes, with corn and
                onion, 96
        soup, 72–73
Kitchen, as a sacred space. See also
                Holidays, Celtic
        altar, creating, 21–27
        appliances, personalizing,
                17–19
        cleaning, 10–15, 129
        creating power spot in, 15–17
        organizing, 17
        parties in, 20–21
Kitchen, decorating, 9–10, 20
        in Autumn, 41–44
        for Samhain, 68–69
        in Spring, 128–31
        in Summer, 169–70
        in Winter, 83–87
Kitchen Goddess Feasts, 27–28, 55,
        94
Lammas, 193–94
Lavender, 13
Leeks
        and potatoes, gratin, 122–23
        soup, 72–73
Lemon peel, 13
Lentils, 76–77
Lovable Lentils in Pumpkin Bowls,
        76–77
Magic Isle Pasties, 142–43
Mama Zabetta's Spicy Stir-Fried
        Greens, 201–2

Maple Candy, 153–54
Marjoram, 13, 76
Maura's Irish Soda Bread, 138
Meditations
        onion, 179–81
        peach, 181–82
        pomegranate, 55, 56–58
        potato, 100–3
        scrying, 69–71
        sprouting, 132–35
Midsummer Marinades, 187–88
Midsummer Salad, 185
Millet, 200
Moony Apple Pie, 77
Mugwort, 70–71
Mushrooms, omelet, 152–53
Native Americans, 50
New Potatoes with Dill, 151–52
Nuts
        hazelnuts, 48–49
        and salad, 47
        and sauces, 63
        toasted, 161
Onion
        meditation, 179–81
        skillet cakes, 96
Oranges, salad, 109
Peach
        meditation, 181–82
        pie, 203
Pears, baked, 52–53
Peas, soup, 171–72
Peppermint, 13
Persephone, 54–55, 58
Persephone Salad, 61
Persephone's Autumn Dressing, 62

Pie
    apple, 77–78
    fruit (dried), 124–25
    peach, 203
    pumpkin, 97–98
    Savory Yuletide Pie, 111–13
    vegetable, 111–13
Pie crust
    Graham cracker, 204
    non-dairy, 78
    wholemeal, 176–77
Plum Pudding, 114–16
Pomander Dressing, 110
Pomander Salad, 109
Pomegranate meditation, 55, 56–58
Potatoes
    with dill, 151–52
    with leeks, gratin, 122–23
    meditation, 100–3
    roasted, 95
Prunes, pudding, 114–16
Pudding
    plum, 114–15
    pumpkin, 97–98
Pumpkin
    how to cook, 89–91
    pie, 97–98
    pudding, 97–98
    soup, 92–93
Quiche, 175–76
    crust for, 176–77
Raspberries, 191
Real Earth-Mother Whole Grain
    Bread, 194–95
Rice
    and beans, 189–90

Risotto Primavera, 161–62
Risotto Primavera, 161–62
Root Soup, 108–9
Rooted Winter Salads, 120–21
Rosemary, 13
Sage, 13–14
Salads
    apple, 61, 73
    flowers in, 172–73
    and nuts, 47, 93–94, 150
    oranges, 109
    Pomander Salad, 109
    Persephone Salad, 61
    Rooted Winter Salads, 120–21
    seeds in, 199
    Spring Greens Salad, 142
    sprouts, 141, 150
    wild greens, 158–59
    Winter Greens and Walnuts,
        93–94
Salads, dressings for
    Autumn Cider Dressing, 74
    Persephone's Autumn Dressing,
        62
    Pomander Dressing, 110
    Simple Summer Dressing, 173
    Ume Plum Dressing, 151
Samhain, 43, 68–72, 73, 77
Sauces
    Creamy Cashew Sauce, 63
    marinades, 187–88
Savory Yuletide Pie, 111–13
Scrying Brew, 69–71
Sea salt, 14
Seeds, 199
Shuck Bread, 196–97

Simple-Gifts Millet, 200
Simple Strawberry Shortcake,
    177–78
Simple Summer Dressing, 173
Smoky Pumpkin Soup, 92–93
Soups
    apple–squash, 46
    bean, 118–20
    Cailleach (kale–leek), 72–73
    cherry, 184
    Demeter's Soothing Oat-Bread
        Soup, 59–60
    miso, 149–50
    pea, 171–72
    pumpkin, 92–93
    spinach, 157–58
    tomato, 198–99
    vegetable, 108–9, 139–41
    Spinach, soup, 157–58
Spring, 128–32
    Beltane, 32, 156
    Imbolc, 136–37
    recipes for, 138–64
    Spring Equinox, 146–48
Spring Equinox, 146–48
Spring Greens Salad, 142
Spring Supper Omelet with
    Mushrooms, 152–53
Sprouted Spring Salads, 141
Sprouts
    growing, 134–35
    meditation, 132–35
Squash
    roasted, 95
    soup, 46
    stew, 50

Stuffed Acorn Squash, 64
Squirrels, 47
St. Joan's Wort, 14
Stew, 50–51
Strawberries, shortcake, 177–78
Stuffed Acorn Squash, 64
Summer, 168–71
    Lammas, 193–94
    recipes for, 171–204
    Summer Solstice, 182–83
Summer Solstice, 182–83
Sunna, 203
Sunny Peach Pie, 203
Sweet Potato–Apple Bake, 75
Tarts, corn with greens and hazel-
    nuts, 48–49
Tea
    herbal, 12–14

white pine, 105–6
Thousand-Names Bean Soup,
    118–20
Three Sisters Harvest Stew, 50–51
Titania's Cherry Soup, 184
Toasted Tamari Almonds, 161
Tomato Venus Soup, 198–99
Turnovers, vegetable, 142–43
Ukemochi Miso Soup, 149–50
Ume Plum Dressing, 151
Vanilla, 14
Vegetables
    grilled, 186–89
    marinades for, 187–88
    pie, 111–13
    roasted, 94–95
    salad, 120–21
    soup, 108–9, 139–41

stir-fried, 201–2
turnovers, 142–43
Vegetarian diet, 2
Venus, 198
Waking Earth Cake, 144–45
Wassail, 106–7
White Pine Tea, 105–6
Wild Salad, 158–59
Winter, 82–89
recipes for, 91–125
Winter Solstice, 84, 103–8
Winter Fruit Pies, 124–25
Winter Greens and Walnuts Salad,
    93–94
Winter Solstice, 84, 103–8
Winter Sunset Carrots, 122